The Book of
Elton John
Guitar
& Bass

Exclusive Distributor for the UK:

Music Sales Limited, Distribution Centre, Newmarket Road, Bury St Edmunds, Suffolk IP33 3YB, UK.

Typeset in Glasgow and Minion.

Printed in The Netherlands.

ISBN 978-1-84772-074-0

Order No. AM990495

www.musicsales.com

Hugo Pinksterboer

Tipbook
Electric
Guitar
& Bass

Handy, clearly written, and up-to-date.
The **reference manual for both beginners and**
advanced electric guitarists and bassists, including
Tipcodes and a glossary.

Wise Publications
part of The Music Sales Group

London • New York • Paris • Sydney • Copenhagen • Berlin • Madrid • Tokyo

Thanks

For their information, their expertise, their time, and their help we'd like to thank the following musicians, teachers, technicians, and other guitar and bass experts: Elliot Freedman, Stephen White (Guitar Tech, CA), Anderson Page (Modulus Guitars, CA), Wouter Zimmerman (Electric Sound), Henny van Ochten (Texas & Tweed), John van der Veer, Keith Brawley (Brawley Guitars, CA), Ron Knotter, Will Vermeer, Davina Cowan, Mark Zandveld, Gerard Braun, Wim Dijkgraaf, the late Willy Heijnen, Jos Kamphuis, Heino Hoekema, Frans van Ingen, Jean Zijta, Edwin Dijkman and Sander Ruijg, Harm van der Geest, Chris Teerlink and Martin van de Lucht (Luthiers Guitars), Anno Galema, Ulbo de Sitter, Harold Koenders and Tom Keverkamp, Harry de Jonge and everyone else at Sacksioni Guitars, and the guitar specialists at Vox Humana. We also wish to thank Ron Knotter for his musical help in making the Tipcode-movies.

Anything missing?

Any omissions? Any areas that could be improved? Please go to www.tipbook.com to contact us; thanks!

The makers

Journalist, writer, and musician **Hugo Pinksterboer**, author of The Tipbook Series, has published hundreds of interviews, articles, and instrument, video, CD, and book reviews for national and international music magazines.

Illustrator, designer, and musician **Gijs Bierenbroodspot** has worked as an art director for a wide variety of magazines and developed numerous ad campaigns. While searching for information about saxophone mouthpieces, he got the idea for this series of books on music and musical instruments. He is responsible for the layout and illustrations of all of the Tipbooks.

Acknowledgements

Concept, design, and illustrations: Gijs Bierenbroodspot
Cover photo: René Vervloet
Editor: Robert L. Doerschuk
Proofreader: Nancy Bishop

IN BRIEF

Have you just started playing? Are you thinking of buying an electric guitar or bass, or do you want to learn more about the one you already have? If so, this book will tell you all you need to know. About the main parts of these instruments, and about lessons and practicing; about choosing and play-testing guitars and basses; about pickups, strings, picks, and straps; about tuning and maintenance; about the instrument's history and family – and much more.

The best you can
Having read this Tipbook, you'll be able to get the most out of your guitar or bass, to buy the best instrument you can, and to easily grasp any other literature on the subject, from magazines to books and Internet publications.

Begin at the beginning
If you have just started playing, or haven't yet begun, pay particular attention to the first four chapters. Have you been playing longer? Then skip ahead to Chapter 5. Please note that all prices mentioned in this book are based on estimated street prices in American dollars.

Glossary
The glossary at the end of the book briefly explains most of the terms you'll come across as a bassist or guitarist. To make life even easier, it doubles as an index.

Hugo Pinksterboer

CONTENTS

SEE WHAT YOU READ WITH TIPCODE

www.tipbook.com

In addition to the many illustrations on the following pages, Tipbooks offer you a new way to see – and even hear – what you are reading about. The *Tipcodes* that you will come across regularly in this book give you access to extra pictures, short movies, soundtracks, and other additional information at www.tipbook.com.

Here is how it works: On page 82 of this book there's a paragraph on fitting new strings. Right above that paragraph it says **Tipcode EGTR-009**. Type in that code on the Tipcode page at www.tipbook.com and you will see a short movie that shows you how to do this. Similar movies are available on a variety of subjects.

Enter code, watch movie
You enter the Tipcode below the movie window on the Tipcode page. In most cases, you will then see the relevant images or hear a soundtrack within five to ten seconds. Tipcodes activate a short movie, sound, or both, or a series of photos.

Tipcodes listed
For your convenience, all the Tipcodes used in this book are shown in a single list on page 136.

Quick start
The movies, photo series, and soundtracks are designed so that they start quickly. If you miss something the first time, you can of course repeat them. And if it all happens too fast, use the pause button below the movie window.

First, make your selection: Tipcode, chords, and fingering charts, or the glossary.

The Tipcode window displays movies, photo series, fingering charts, chords, and explanations of the words used in this book.

Enter a Tipcode here and click on the button. Want to see it again? Click again.

These links take you directly to other interesting sites.

Plug-ins

If the software you need to view the movies or photos is not yet installed on your computer, you'll automatically be told which software you need, and where you can download it. This kind of software (*plug-ins*) is free.

Still more at www.tipbook.com

You can find even more information at www.tipbook.com. For instance, you can look up words in the glossaries of all the Tipbooks published to date. For guitarists and pianists there are chord diagrams and for saxophonists, clarinetists, and flutists there are fingering charts, for drummers there are the rudiments. Also included are links to some of the websites mentioned in the *Want to Know More?* section of each Tipbook.

1. GUITARISTS, BASSISTS?

Guitarists can play anything from scorching solos and power chords to the sweetest notes and smoothest harmonies. Bassists can slap or pop their instruments, or make them growl or sing just as easily. And guitarists and bassists are both indispensable in many, many types of bands.

With an electric guitar or bass you can play numerous musical styles. From heavy metal to surf, from country to R&B, Cajun or klezmer, folk, jazz, funk, Latin, soul, and even classical music.

One or more

You can concentrate on one style, or you can play as many different types of music as you want. And you can do so using a single instrument only, or you can find yourself a different one for each type of sound: There are hundreds of different guitars and basses available, each with its own character.

As different as can be

If you would compare a heavy rock guitarist to a jazz guitarist, you'll see more differences than similarities. They use different instruments, different strings, different playing techniques, different amplifiers – and most probably different picks too.

Bassists too

The same goes for bassists. Some types of music ask for bright, percussive, complex bass patterns, while other bands

Two guitars – as different as can be.

require no more than a subdued low note on every beat. And there are plenty of different instruments available to suit every need and style. This book helps you make a choice.

Chords

Just like keyboard instruments, guitars allow you to play multiple notes simultaneously (*chords*), or play the melody as well as the accompaniment. This turns the instrument into a one-piece band.

Singers

Two similarities between guitarists and keyboard players are that they often write most of the songs of the band's repertoire, and that they're often the singer of the band. Some bassists sing too.

Accompaniment

Most bass players, however, concentrate on building the foundation for the band, closely cooperating with the drummer. There's no base, without a bassist…

Popular instruments

Electric guitars and basses are popular instruments, in part because they're pretty easy to get started on. With just a little bit of talent and determination, you can play your first songs within a couple of weeks.

Affordable
Because they're so popular and so many of them are made, (bass) guitars are quite affordable. For some four hundred dollars or even less you can get yourself a 'gig rig' including an instrument, a small amplifier, a tuner, a strap, a pick, a cable…

Reading music
If you want to play the guitar, you don't need to learn how to read music if you really don't want to. After all, there are quite a few famous guitarists and bassists who can't read a note. On the other hand, it's not that hard to learn, it gives you access to tons of music, and it most certainly broadens your career options.

Young
You can start to learn the bass or guitar at pretty much any age. Special downsized instruments are available for the very youngest players. There's more about them on page 40.

2. A QUICK TOUR

This chapter covers the key parts of electric guitars, basses, and hollow-body guitars, and offers a brief introduction to amps and effects.

The instruments in this book are called electric because you need an 'electric' amplifier to play them. Without an amplifier, you can hardly hear them at all.

Pickups

Electric guitars and basses have *pickups*. These devices literally 'pick up' the strings' vibrations and convert them to electric signals. A cable transports the signals to the amplifier. The amplifier boosts and sends them to the speaker.

Solid bodies

Most electric guitars and basses are *solid-body* instruments: They have a solid body, as opposed to the large, hollow soundbox of an acoustic guitar.

SOLID-BODY ELECTRICS

Solid-body electrics come in an endless variety of shapes and sizes, as you will see in the following chapters.

Pickguard

On many guitars, a *pickguard* protects the body from being scratched by your pick. It's also a cover for the wiring inside the instrument. Solid-body guitars without a pickguard have one or more cover plates on the back.

A solid-body guitar.

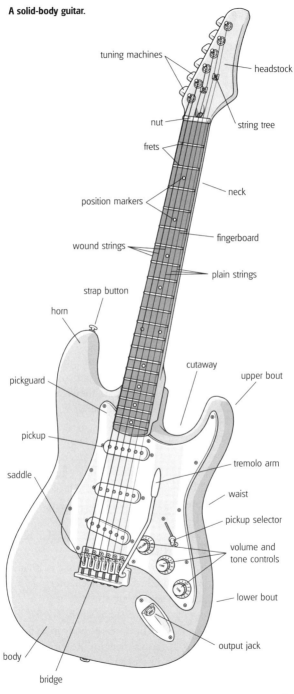

tuning machines

headstock

nut

string tree

frets

neck

position markers

fingerboard

wound strings

plain strings

strap button

horn

cutaway

upper bout

pickguard

pickup

tremolo arm

saddle

waist

pickup selector

volume and
tone controls

lower bout

output jack

body

bridge

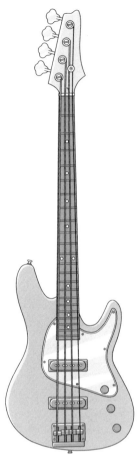

Solid-body bass guitar.

Neck and headstock
The instrument's strings run along the *neck*, from the body to the *headstock*.

Truss rod
Hidden inside the neck is an adjustable *truss rod* that helps counteract the tension of the strings. Some necks have other reinforcements as well.

Fingerboard
The front side of the neck is the *fingerboard* onto which you press your fingers. Pressing a string onto the fingerboard makes the vibrating section of the string shorter. As a result, it will sound higher. This way, you can make any string produce various notes.

Frets
The fingerboard is divided into *positions* by a number of small metal strips, the *frets*. This explains the fingerboard's alternative name, *fretboard*.

Position markers
Position markers show you where you are at the fingerboard. Most instruments have *side dots* or *side fret markers* as well. These are located on the upper side of the fingerboard, so they're easier to see when you're playing.

Fretting strings
Stopping or *fretting* a string in the 5th position is commonly known as playing the string *at the 5th fret*.

Cutaway
To make the highest frets easier to play, most instruments have a *cutaway*: The body is recessed where it meets the

neck. Many guitars and basses have a double cutaway, and thus two *horns*.

Waist

Guitar bodies have hips (the *lower bout*) and shoulders (the *upper bout*). In between is the *waist*, which is either symmetrical or offset.

Binding

Instruments with an *arched top* often have a decorative and protective strip running along the edges of the body. This *binding* sometimes extends to the neck and the headstock as well.

STRINGS

Most guitars have six strings; most basses have four.

E, A, D, G, B, E   Tipcode EGTR-001

If you start at the thickest, lowest string, the six guitar strings are tuned to the notes E, A, D, G, B, E.

Memory joggers

This sequence can be easily memorized as **E**ating **A**nd **D**rinking **G**ive **B**rain **E**nergy, **E**ating **A**nd **D**rinking **G**ives **B**elly **E**xpansion, or **E**ven **A**dam **D**id **G**et **B**ored **E**ventually.

String numbers

The six strings have numbers too. Confusingly, they're numbered the other way around: The thin, high-sounding E-string is referred to as the *first string*. As a reminder: The thinnest string has the 'thinnest' number, the 1.

Wound strings

On most electric guitars, the three thickest strings are wound with metal wire. The extra mass of the metal winding helps these *wound strings* to sound as low as they should. The three thinnest strings (B and E) are *plain strings*.

Bass strings   Tipcode EGTR-002

The strings of a bass guitar have the same note names as the four lowest guitar strings: E, A, D, G, from thick to thin. They sound an octave lower than the guitar strings.

(An octave is eight white notes on a piano, as you can see below.)

Twice as thick

To make the bass strings sound that much lower, they're about twice as thick as the corresponding guitar strings, and a lot longer. All bass strings are wound strings.

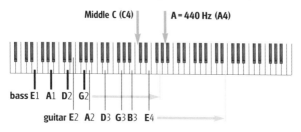

The four strings of an electric bass are tuned an octave lower than the four lowest guitar strings. A=440 (key A4) is the pitch most instruments are tuned to (see page 97).

Numbered octaves

As you can see, the octaves are numbered. The low E-string on a guitar is E2; low E on a bass is E1, an octave lower.

HARDWARE

The metal parts of a guitar are known as the *hardware*.

Tuning machines

The strings are tuned with the *tuning machines*, which are also known as *tuning gears*, *tuners*, (*tuning*) *pegs*, or *machine heads*.

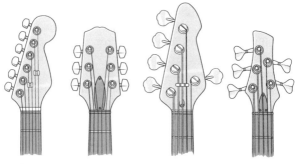

Different tuning machine arrangements: two guitars (left) and two five-string basses (right).

Nut

Between the head and the fingerboard, the strings run through the slots in the *nut*. This helps to keep the strings properly spaced.

Bridge

From the nut, the strings run along the fingerboard, past the pickups, toward the *bridge*.

Saddles

At the bridge, each string runs over a *saddle*. These saddles can be used to adjust the instrument. Most types of bridges have one saddle per string.

Tailpiece

The strings are attached either to the bridge or to a separate *stopbar tailpiece*.

Tremolo system   Tipcode EGTR-003

Many guitars have a *tremolo system* or *trem*. Moving the trem arm makes all the strings go down – or up – in pitch simultaneously, which allows for pitch bend and vibrato effects.

PICKUPS AND CONTROLS

Most guitars have two or three pickups; most basses have one or two.

Bridge and neck pickups

If you play the strings close to the bridge, you'll get a brighter, edgier sound than if you play them close to the neck. Likewise, the pickup that's closest to the bridge produces a brighter, edgier sound than the *neck pickup* – even if they're exactly the same pickups.

Selector

On guitars, the *pickup selector* allows you to choose which pickup(s) you use, so you can vary your sound.

Balance

Basses often have a *balance control*, so you can blend the sound of the bridge and neck pickups, or use just one of them.

Volume controls

Some instruments have two *volume controls*, rather than one. These controls can also be used to mix the sound of two pickups.

Tone

The *tone control(s)* can be used to make the sound a bit darker, warmer, or less bright.

Output jack

The signal produced by the pickups goes to the amp through a *cable*, which connects to the instrument's *output jack* or *output socket*.

HOLLOW-BODY ELECTRICS

Compared to solidbodies, *hollow-body electric guitars* produce a warmer, mellower, or rounder sound.

The top

Most hollow-body instruments have an arched top – hence their other name, *archtops*. These tops usually have two *f*-shaped soundholes, just like a violin.

Floating bridge

Hollowbodies typically have a one-piece *floating bridge*, held in place only by the pressure of the strings. The tailpiece and pickguard are also floating designs.

Feedback

Hollow-body instruments are very susceptible to *feedback*. This is the loud *skreee* you also hear if you accidentally point a microphone at a loudspeaker. To reduce feedback, most shallower models have a solid wooden block built into the soundbox. This block also improves the sustain of the instrument. Such guitars are often used by blues and fusion players.

Many (many) names

The many different names used for shallow hollow-body instruments, with or without a center block, are quite confusing. They range from *semi-solid* to *semi-hollow*, and from *thinline* to *slimline* – and there are no set definitions.

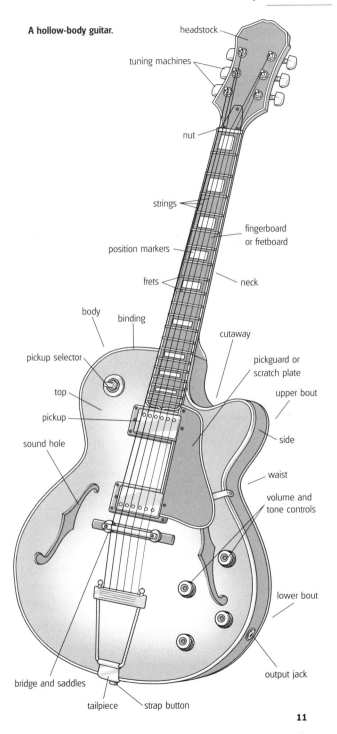

A hollow-body guitar.

headstock

tuning machines

nut

strings

fingerboard or fretboard

position markers

frets

neck

body

binding

cutaway

pickup selector

pickguard or scratch plate

top

upper bout

pickup

side

sound hole

waist

volume and tone controls

lower bout

bridge and saddles

output jack

tailpiece

strap button

LEFT-HANDED INSTRUMENTS

Right-handed bassists and guitarists play the strings with their right hand, and they fret them with their left. Many left-handed players do it the other way around. As righties outnumber lefties, most shops store just a limited number of 'left-handed instruments.' Some companies charge a higher price for them; others don't.

Other solutions

On left-handed instruments, everything is 'the other way around.' If not, the trem arm and the controls would be in an awkward place, the strings would go from high to low rather than from low to high, and instruments with a single cutaway would have this useful recession on the wrong side.

A 'left-handed' solidbody.

AMPLIFIERS

Most guitarists and bass players use a *combo amplifier:* an amplifier and one or more speakers in one unit.

Character

An amplifier does a lot more than just boosting sound. It also lends a certain character or color to it: If you play your guitar through different amps, it'll sound different each time. And just as there are special guitars for certain styles of music, some types of amps are better suited for heavy metal, and others for jazz, for example.

Speakers

The speaker or speakers used with the amp play a major role in the sound too. After all, when you play amplified, the speaker is the part that produces the sound.

Two parts

The actual amplifier is made up of a *preamplifier* and a *power amp.* The preamp is used to manipulate the sound with volume, tone, and other controls. The power amp, as its name indicates, supplies the power.

Gain

In addition to one or more volume controls, most amplifiers have a *gain* control. On many guitar amps, you use this control to set the amount of distortion you want.

Two channels   Tipcode EGTR-004

Most modern guitar amps have two *channels.* You use the clean, normal, or rhythm channel for a clean, undistorted sound. Most players use this channel when they play chords. The second channel is the one you use for a lighter or heavier distorted solo sound. It's known as the drive, overdrive, lead, or crunch channel.

Controls and footswitch

Each channel has its own volume control, and it's good to have separate tone controls for each channel too. Two-channel amps usually come with a *footswitch* that allows you to change channels from a distance.

Gain for basses

On bass amps, the gain control is not usually used to set the amount of distortion (most bassists use a clean sound), but to adjust the amp to the signal strength of the bass: Some basses have a much stronger signal than others.

Solid state or tubes

Amplifiers use either *transistors (solid state amplifiers)* or *tubes* for the actual amplification of the signal. Many players favor the more expensive tube amps for what's often described as a warmer, fatter type of sound. Besides these two basic types of amps, there are hybrid models – *e.g.,* with a tube preamp and a solid state power amp.

Modeling amps

Modeling amps use digital technology to emulate the sound of well-known amplifiers of various makes. This type of amp usually features a wide variety of effects too.

Power

A major factor when buying an amp is what *power rating* to go for. For home practicing purposes, a small 10- or 15-watt amp will usually do. For performances in small venues you'll soon need some 50 to 100 watts. Bass amps usually have a higher power rating than the amp of the guitarist in the same band: Low frequencies require more energy and thus more watts to be properly amplified.

There's more

Contrary to general belief, the power rating of an amp doesn't tell you how loud it can sound *per se*; there are many more factors that come into play. *Tipbook Amps & Effects* (check www.tipbook.com) will tell you the entire story.

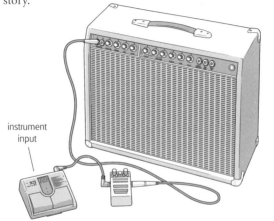

instrument input

An amplifier, a programmable multi-effect processor, and a traditional effect pedal.

EFFECTS

Most guitarists and many bass players use one or more effects to 'color' their sound. Amplifiers often have one or two effects built in, and sometimes more than that. You can expand your possibilities by adding *effect pedals* or *multi-effect processors* to your gear.

Reverb

Reverb is one of the most common effects. It makes your sound bigger, adding lots of space to it. Most guitar amps come with a built-in reverb.

Distortion

As mentioned above, you can generate a distorted guitar sound by turning up the gain on your amplifier. Alternatively, you can use a separate distortion pedal. Why would you? For one thing, because – just like amps, or guitars – *distortion* effects can have very different timbres, and you will like one more than the other. The names of the various distortion pedals (Metal, Smokin', Grunge, Grilled Cheese…) clearly illustrate that.

Other effects
Tipcode EGTR-005

Some other popular effects are *chorus* (makes your sound a bit fuller by doubling it at slightly varying pitches), *delay* (repeats the notes you play), and *wah-wah* (does exactly what its name sounds like).

Effect pedals

The traditional effect pedals usually have a footswitch to turn the effect on and off, and three or more controls. On a delay pedal, for example, you can set the volume of the effect, how long you will hear the effect, how often the notes are repeated, and the delay time – from thousandths of a second (making you sound just a bit 'thicker') to a whole second or more (so you can play over the top of what you just played).

Multi effects

A multi-effect processor is a single unit that contains a number of effects, which can be mixed or used individually. Most have a number of pedals and a programming section, so you can design your sounds at home and have them available onstage by the flick of a pedal. They often feature a built-in metronome (see page 20), a tuner (see page 95), and a headphone jack so you can use it for silent practice too. Effects and multi effect processors or *signal processors* are also sold in rack-mountable units.

Combined

Effect pedals and multi effects can be combined. In the setup on the previous page, you have to plug your instrument cable into the multi-effect unit. The guitar signal is first processed by the multi effect, and then by the effect pedal. The pedal is connected to the amp's instrument input.

3. LEARNING TO PLAY

Guitars and basses are among the easiest instruments to get started on. With just a little talent and practice you can get yourself to play some basic songs in just a few weeks. Learning to play these instruments really well and make them sound good takes a lot more time, of course, and you can easily spend a lifetime learning to really master them.

You can play numerous rock and pop songs on guitar as soon as you've mastered a few basic chords. Learning these chords is a matter of studying *chord charts*: diagrams that indicate simply where to put your fingers for each chord.

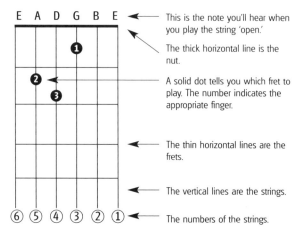

E A D G B E ← This is the note you'll hear when you play the string 'open.'

The thick horizontal line is the nut.

A solid dot tells you which fret to play. The number indicates the appropriate finger.

The thin horizontal lines are the frets.

The vertical lines are the strings.

⑥ ⑤ ④ ③ ② ① ← The numbers of the strings.

This chord chart shows the E-major chord. Play string 3 at the first fret with your index finger, play string 5 at the second fret with your middle finger, and play string 4 at the second fret with your ring finger.

Books and digital devices

Many songbooks include charts of the chords you need for each song. Also, there are books that have charts of the various types of chords and, as an alternative, there are miniature digital devices that can display hundreds of different chords at the touch of a button or two. Chord charts can be found on the Internet as well.

Tablature: for basses too

Guitar solos and bass lines can be put on paper without using regular notes too. This is done using the *tablature* or *tab system*, shown below. Many songbooks include tab notation. Tablature doesn't allow for precise rhythmical notation, so regular notes are often included as well.

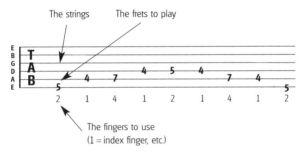

The tablature staff represents a guitar or bass neck. This bass line can be played on guitars and basses.

Reading music

Chord charts and tablature offer an easy way to learn to play an instrument without having to read music in the traditional sense. Still, it's not a bad idea to learn how to read regular notation too.

- Regular notation gives you access to **loads of books and magazines** with exercises, songs, and solos.
- It'll provide you with **better insight** into the way chords and songs are structured.
- It enables you to **put down on paper** your own songs, solos, ideas, and exercises – not just for (bass) guitarists, but for other musicians as well
- It enables you to read parts that were **not written for (bass) guitarists**.
- It makes you **more of a musician**, instead of 'just' a (bass) guitarist.

- As it **widens the range of gigs** you can play, it broadens your career options – both as an amateur and as a pro.
- And finally: **It isn't that hard at all**. *Tipbook Music on Paper – Basic Theory* (see page 142) teaches you the basics within a few chapters.

LESSONS

Even while there are so many – successful – self-taught players, consulting a teacher isn't a bad idea either. Getting the basics down helps you to start out the right way, and if you find yourself stuck in your learning process later on, a good teacher will help you to get going again.

The right teacher

If you take a little bit of time, you'll be able to find a teacher who's willing and able to teach you the style of music you want to play, be it pop, jazz, or punk.

More than just how to play

Good teachers teach you more than just how to play chords and solos. They'll teach you technique, how to produce a good tone, good posture, and practice and tuning routines, for example, and they may introduce you to different styles of music.

Questions, questions

On your first visit to a teacher, don't just ask how much it costs. Here are some other questions.

- Is an **introductory lesson** included? This is a good way to find out how well you get on with the teacher, and for that matter, with the instrument.
- Is the teacher interested in taking you on as a student even if you are doing it **just for the fun of it**, or will he or she expect you to practice at least three hours a day?
- Do you have to make a large investment in method books right away, or is the **course material provided**?
- Can you **record your lessons**, so that you can listen again to how you sounded and what was said when you get home?
- Will you be allowed to concentrate fully on **the style of music you want to play**, or will you be required to learn other styles? Will you be stimulated to do so?

Finding a teacher

Looking for a private teacher? Music stores may have teachers on their staff, or be able to refer you to one. You can also consult your local Musician's Union, or the band director at a high school. Do check the classified ads in newspapers, in music magazines or on supermarket bulletin boards, or consult the *Yellow Pages*. Professional private teachers will usually charge between twenty-five and seventy-five dollars per hour. Some make house calls, for which you'll pay extra.

Group or individual lessons

While most students take individual lessons, you can also try group lessons if that's an option in your area. Private lessons are more expensive but can be tailored exactly to your needs.

Collectives

You may want to check whether there are any teacher collectives or music schools in your vicinity. These collectives usually offer extras such as playing in bands, master classes, and clinics, in a wide variety of styles and at various levels.

Acoustic lessons

Many electric players studied the acoustic guitar as well, and your 'electric sound' may benefit from 'acoustic lessons.' How come? For one thing, because it takes more effort to make an acoustic instrument sound really good – so being able to make an acoustic guitar sound good can easily improve your tone on an electric one.

PRACTICING

You can learn to play without reading notes. Without a teacher too. But you can't do without practicing.

How long?

How long you need to practice depends on what you want to achieve. Many top musicians practiced four to eight hours a day for several years, or more. The more time you spend on it, the faster you improve. Half an hour a day usually results in steady progress.

Three times ten

If you find it hard to practice half an hour a day, try dividing it up into two quarter-hour sessions, or three of ten minutes each.

Books, videos, and more

Guitarists and bassists have easy access to tons of practice and reading material:

- There are **bass and guitar books** for absolute beginners and absolute pros. Quite a few of them have a tape or CD with examples or play-along exercises; you turn off the sound of the (bass) guitarist and play that part yourself.
- Most **guitar magazines** include lessons, charts, and other educational stuff.
- **Instructional videos** can be very helpful. They're available for many styles and all levels.
- There's **software** that turns your computer into a guitar or bass teacher.
- The **Internet** can help you improve your playing too: Some websites even include free lessons (see page 139).

Keeping time

Most songs are supposed to be played at a steady tempo. Practicing with a *metronome* helps you to do so. A metronome is a small mechanical or electronic device that ticks or beeps out a steady, adjustable pulse, which helps you to work on your tempo, timing, and rhythm.

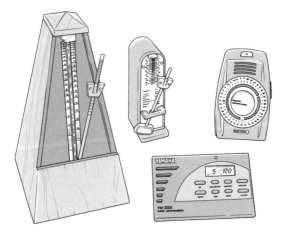

Two mechanical metronomes and two electronic ones.

Drum machines and more

A drum machine is a great alternative to the metronome. There are similar machines that can play programmable bass lines or guitar chords too, and some can sound like a full band that you can play along with. *Phrase trainers* are devices that can slow down a musical phrase from a CD, for example, so you can figure out even the meanest, fastest licks at your own tempo. There is software available that does the same thing.

Record yourself

It's hard to really listen to yourself while you're playing. That's why many musicians record their practice sessions. A Walkman with a built-in microphone is basically all you need, but you'll get better results if you use better equipment. For example, some guitar amps can be hooked up directly to a recording machine – be it a minidisk recorder, a cassette recorder, or your computer.

No noise

One of the many nice things about electric guitars and basses is that you can practice for hours without bothering anyone. First of all, there are plenty of things you can practice without using an amplifier at all. Or you can get yourself a special Walkman-sized practice amp, or any other type of amp that comes with a headphone jack. Finally, many effect processors have built-in *amplifier simulations.* Plug in your instrument, plug in a pair of headphones, select your favorite virtual amp and effects, and wail. If you use headphones, keep the volume down to prevent hearing damage.

Hearing damage

Many bands play and practice at volumes that can cause hearing damage pretty easily, so do consider using some kind of hearing protection. As hearing loss is usually noticed only when it's too late, prevention is the key. Really.

Cheap or expensive earplugs...

The cheapest foam plastic earplugs, available from most music stores and drugstores, will make your band sound as if it's playing next door. The most expensive earplugs are custom-made to fit your ears. These plugs often have adjustable filters that reduce the volume without affecting the sound.

... and in between

Plastic earplugs come in many variations. Some just reduce the overall volume; others make the band sound dull and far away, just like earmuffs do. Also, some are easier to clean than others. Ask fellow musicians (drummers!) for their experiences with hearing protection, and don't hesitate to try different products until you find the ones that really fit and work for you. A hearing aid will cost more in the long run, and ringing ears (*tinnitus*) never stop ringing.

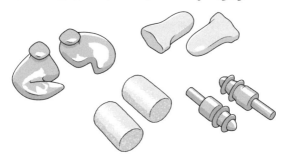

Some affordable types of earplugs.

Get to work

Finally, visit as many concerts as you can. One of the best ways to learn to play is seeing other musicians at work. Living legends or local amateurs – every gig's a learning experience. And the very best way to learn to play? Play a lot!

4. BUYING A (BASS) GUITAR

You can get a brand new electric guitar and an amp for very little money – and you can just as easily spend thousands of dollars. The same goes for basses and bass amps. This chapter tells the basics about prices, stores, buying new or secondhand, and where to get product information. Chapters 5, 6, and 8 deal with what to pay attention to once you're in a store.

Some hundred fifty to two hundred dollars is all you need to get yourself a brand new solid-body electric, and a small practice amp should cost about the same. Bass guitars usually cost a little more than guitars of the same quality.

Packages
Many stores offer complete packages: (bass) guitar, amp, cable, pick, electronic tuner, and gig bag. These packages are available from around four hundred dollars, and sometimes even less.

The very cheapest
Teachers often advise against buying the very cheapest instruments. As with any other product, you can't expect a lot of quality for little money. Still, you can have years of musical fun with a budget guitar.

Hard to spot
It can be hard to spot the differences between budget, midrange, and expensive basses and guitars, especially for beginning players. Most affordable instruments look as if

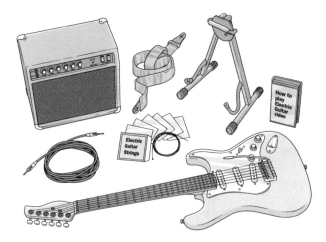

... for some four hundred dollars...

they should cost a lot more than they do – and some also sound much better than their price suggests!

Four or more
A solid-body instrument that sounds, tunes, and plays well enough to be used on gigs can be yours for as little as three to four hundred dollars. Hollow-body guitars are more expensive than solidbodies of similar quality.

Amps and effects
If you're going to play gigs and need to bring your own amp, be prepared to spend some five hundred to a thousand dollars – and again, you can go much higher. Most guitarists also use one or more effects. Effect pedals start around fifty dollars, and multi-effect processors at around three times that price.

Better, better, better
Spending more on a guitar buys you better wood, hardware, pickups, workmanship, and quality control, to mention some of the main points. Their combined result is an instrument that can be expected to sound better, play better, last longer, and have a higher resale value – and you may just enjoy it a lot more than a cheap one too... Usually, more money also buys you more options: more colors to choose from, various pickup configurations, and so on.

Custom-made

If you want to have even more options, you can have an instrument custom-made. Several guitar brands have custom shops, and there are many one-man factories and guitar and bass workshops around. Hand-made instruments usually start around two to three thousand dollars, and go up to ten times that price – or more.

Adjustments

No matter how good an instrument is, it'll never play well and sound good until it has been properly tuned and adjusted. Unfortunately, this is not always the case with the instruments on display. An experienced player can help you tell the badly adjusted instruments from the ones you really shouldn't buy.

THE STORE

The more instruments a store has on display, the harder it is to choose. On the other hand, as selecting (bass) guitars is largely a matter of comparing them, a wide selection is exactly what you need. It's equally important to find salespeople who enjoy their work and know what they're talking about. One more tip? Visit several music stores, and talk to various salespeople, as they all have their own 'sound' too.

Time

Take your time when buying an instrument – you'll probably have to live with it for years. On the other hand, many players ended up buying that one guitar they liked straightaway, after just the first few notes.

Take someone along

If you just started playing, it'll be hard if not impossible to judge an instrument. The best advice is to take a more experienced player along when you go shopping, or select stores where they have musicians on staff.

Buying online

You can also buy your guitar online or by mail order. This makes it impossible to compare instruments, of course, but most online and mail-order companies offer a return service for most or all of their products: If you're not happy with it, you can return it within a certain period of time. Of course the instrument should be in new condition when you send it back.

SECONDHAND

If you don't want to spend too much, but you don't want to play the cheapest instrument either, you may consider buying secondhand. Used instruments by well-known brands often sell for more than equally good ones from lesser-known makes. You may want to take that into account when you buy a new one too.

Privately or in a store?

Purchasing a used instrument from a private party may be cheaper than buying the same one from a store. One of the advantages of buying a used guitar in a store, though, is that you can go back if you have questions. Also, some music stores may offer you a limited warranty on your purchase. Another difference is that a good dealer won't usually ask an outrageous price, but a private seller might – because he doesn't know any better, or because he thinks that you don't.

Vintage guitars

Many players favor older instruments, made in the 1960s, the 1950s, or before, because of their tone, their looks, or their history, because they're rare, or all of the above. Such vintage instruments can easily fetch a higher price than a new one of similar quality.

MORE, MORE

If you want to know all there is to know, stock up on guitarists' and bassists' magazines that offer reviews of the latest gear, and on all the brochures and catalogs you can find. Besides containing a wealth of information, the latter are designed to make you want to spend more than you have, or have in mind – so ask for a price list too. The Internet is another good source for up-to-date product information. And of course there are loads of other specialized books as well. You can find more about these resources on pages 137–139.

5. A GOOD INSTRUMENT

Guitars and basses come in numerous designs, sporting different shapes and sounds, dimensions, wood types, pickup configurations, necks, frets, strings, and so on, and so on. The knowledge presented in the following chapter will help you make a choice, covering pretty much everything there is to look at and to listen for.

How a (bass) guitar sounds depends not only on the instrument itself and on the person who plays it, but also on the strings, the picks, the cables you're using, and of course on your amp and effects. Strings, picks, and cables are explored in Chapters 6 and 7 respectively. Amplifiers and effects will be covered in a Tipbook by that title.

This chapter
After exploring the various body finishes and types, this chapter covers the neck and fingerboard (page 33), the scale (string length; page 40), the frets (41), the tuning machines (44), the bridge (46), tremolos (49), pickups (53), tips on play-testing (67), and buying secondhand instruments (70).

Many variations
Few instruments come in as many designs as electric guitars and basses. Some are extremely versatile, created to be used in a wide variety of musical styles. Others are built for a specific type of music. Often their looks alone will tell: A heavy metal guitar looks very different from one that was designed for country music.

Surf on metal

Though you can play surf music on a guitar that was built for heavy metal, it's usually better to use instruments for the style of music the designer had in mind. Likewise, knowing which guitar your favorite musician is playing can be a useful guide in finding your own.

Differing opinions

Musicians rarely agree about anything. The following chapters won't tell you who is right, or what is best, but rather how different experts think about different issues. You'll discover whom you agree with only by playing, and by listening to guitars or basses – and to the people who play them.

THE BODY

Guitar bodies can be finished with a single solid color; a natural, transparent lacquer; a two- or three-color sunburst finish; or with many other types and styles of finishes.

A sunburst finish.

Plastic or natural

Most instruments have a polyurethane finish. This is a hard and durable synthetic type of lacquer. Natural finishes, such as nitrocellulose or oil, are typically used on more expensive instruments. These organic finishes, which tend to get darker with age, help bring out the instrument's resonance.

Pickguard

Pickguards come in lots of different colors and designs too. Laminated pickguards that show their three white-black-white plies at the edge are very popular. Most of today's pickguards are plastic. Unlike the traditional pickguard material (*i.e.*, celluloid) they don't warp or expand.

Hardware

The hardware is usually black, shiny or matte chrome-plated, or gold-plated. On many instruments, the pickups or pickup covers match the hardware.

Aged
Vintage guitars and basses are so popular that some companies even offer brand-new 'vintage' instruments – artificially aged, with intentionally rusted hardware, discolored plastic parts, and damaged finishes.

SOLID BODIES
The type of wood used for the body affects the instrument's sound and weight. The body's shape influences both looks and balance.

Chipboard or solid wood
The very cheapest guitars often have a chipboard or plywood body. A body that consists of one or more pieces of solid wood helps produce more sustain and a richer sound.

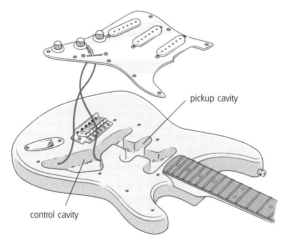

pickup cavity

control cavity

Solid guitar body with cavities for the pickups and controls.

Different wood, different sound
Generally speaking, denser types of wood promote a brighter tone and more sustain than lighter types of wood. That said, many types of wood come in different variations and qualities. Also, the way a guitar is built can completely alter some characteristics, and experts don't always agree when it comes to describing the effect of certain types of

wood. The message? Always listen to the instrument, rather than relying on wood names.

Light or heavy
Poplar, basswood, and alder are three lighter types of wood. They're often said to help produce a warmer, fuller, fatter type of sound. Maple, at the other end of the spectrum, is very dense, and thus makes for a brighter tone.

Weights and densities
Mahogany and ash come in various weights and densities. The lighter types, again, enhance a warmer, mellower tone. Denser variations promote a brighter, 'airier,' more open type of sound. Swamp ash is one of the lighter types of ash.

The top
Because of its beautiful appearance, maple is often used as top wood. It's available in many variations (*i.e.*, quilted maple, bird's eye maple, and flamed or figured maple).

Choosing
There are companies that offer a selection of ten, fifteen, or even more types of wood. When it comes to such choices, looks often play a larger role than sound. Likewise, with some instruments the wood you get depends on the finish you want.

Photo finish
On lower-budget instruments, the 'wooden' top you see isn't real wood. It's a photo that is glued to the instrument and then finished over. It takes an expert eye to distinguish this photo flame contact paper from the real thing, which has more depth and character (in sound too!).

Synthetic bodies
Bodies can also be made entirely of synthetics. Some players praise their consistency; others miss the depth and warmth caused by the natural inconsistencies of wood.

Thick
The size and shape of the body influences sound, weight, and playing comfort. Generally speaking, a thicker, heavier body increases the sustain and makes a richer sound.

Weight

A 'heavy' solidbody can outweigh a light one by three or four pounds – a difference that feels a lot more obvious after an hour's playing.

Balance

The balance is just as important. A neck-heavy guitar can be more tiresome to play than one that actually weighs more, but has a better balance. An uncomfortable balance can sometimes be cured, for example by relocating the strap buttons. A tip: If you usually play standing up, play-test instruments that way too.

Solid?

Not all solidbodies are as solid as they look. Some have one or more invisible sound chambers that reduce the weight and make for a warmer tone. Their names (*chambered bodies* or *semi-hollow bodies*) are also used for shallow-body guitars that clearly show their sound chamber through a soundhole in the top.

Contoured bodies

Today, most instruments have contoured bodies with rounded edges. These designs don't dig in your chest the way some old-style non-contoured *slab* bodies may do.

The heel

The accessibility of the highest frets depends on the depth of the cutaway, but also on the *heel*, where the neck meets the body. The less pronounced the heel is, the less it'll be in your way when reaching for the highest notes. A thicker heel,

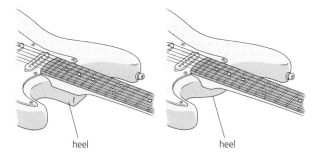

The right-hand design allows for easier access to the highest frets.

on the other hand, is said to make for a more solid, full-bodied sound – just like a heavier body or a thicker neck.

HOLLOWBODIES

Hollow-body instruments come with shallow and deep bodies, with one or two cutaways, with or without a center block, and in various types of wood.

Jazz

Traditionally, jazz players favor a big-box guitar or jazz box. These instruments are often 17" wide at the lower bout, and about 3.5" to 4.5" deep. (This dimension is known as the *rim thickness*).

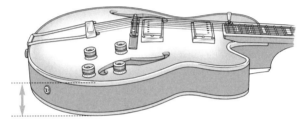

The rim thickness of a jazz guitar.

Shallow with block

The deeper the body is, the more sensitive it is to feedback. This explains why guitarists in loud bands usually opt for shallower models. These guitars often come with a built-in center block that reduces feedback even more, and enhances the sustain too.

Hollow-body top

The top is one of the most fundamental parts of a hollow-body guitar. A solid spruce top is usually said to provide the warmest, deepest, most acoustic type of sound. A maple top makes for a brighter tone. Laminated and pressed arched tops tend to produce a shallower and less dynamic sound than tops that are carved from a solid piece of wood. Solid tops are usually *bookmatched* (see page 124).

Cutaway

Hollow-body cutaways that end in a sharp point are known as Florentine. A Venetian cutaway has a rounded shape.

NECK AND FINGERBOARD

The neck and fingerboard influence both the playability and the sound of the instrument. As with the body, heavier and denser types of wood promote a brighter, richer, more solid sound and sustain. Using more wood (*i.e.*, having a thicker, wider neck) has roughly the same effect.

Thin or thick

'Fast' players often prefer relatively thin necks, as do musicians with small hands. Thicker necks not only feel different, but also enhance the instrument's stability and tone. Rolled, rounded, or beveled edges can make for a more comfortable, broken-in feel.

V, D, C, U

Neck back profiles are often indicated with a letter that resembles their shape. However, the letters used do not always refer to the same types of neck. For example, some players use the letter C for a rounded, smooth-looping, 1960s profile; others use the same letter for thin, low-profile necks. Likewise, some think C and D are similar, while others use D for mid-1980s, square-edge necks. V-type necks have a clearly distinguishable ridge in the middle, and U-necks are very thick.

Different neck thicknesses and profiles, different fingerboards...

Asymmetrical

Asymmetrical necks are rare, but some five- and six-string bass necks are a little fatter under the low B-string.

Width

The neck width is usually measured at the nut. The wider it is, the further apart the strings will be. For fast solos, most players prefer a tighter string spacing. Conversely, clean chords are easier on a wider neck. Slapping bass players usually prefer a wider string spacing than finger-style players, who pluck the strings. Neck widths range from about 1.57" to 1.75" (40–45 mm) on guitars. Bass necks start around 1.5". On some basses, string spacing can be adjusted at the bridge (see page 48).

More strings

Instruments with extra strings (seven-string guitars; basses with five or more strings) usually have wider necks too. For example, most five-string bass necks are between 1.75" and 1.80" at the nut.

Getting used

Extra strings extend your tonal range, and the extra neck wood is said to make for a slightly rounder sound with added mids – but you do need to get used to playing such an instrument, because of both the wider neck and the extra strings. Also, certain playing techniques will always be easier on an instrument with the traditional number of strings.

More strings, more money

Many basses are available in four-, five-, and six-string models. In the lower and intermediate price ranges, an 'extra string' typically costs fifty to a hundred dollars more.

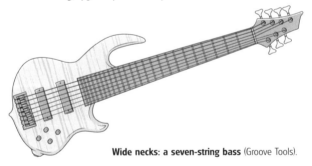

Wide necks: a seven-string bass (Groove Tools).

Radius

If you look along the neck of a (bass) guitar, you'll see that the fingerboard is curved, rising slightly toward the middle strings. The exact curvature is indicated by the *radius*.

More inches, flatter fingerboard

The radius is always given in inches. The higher the figure, the flatter the fingerboard. A 7.25" radius is very curved; a

15" radius is pretty flat. What's best for you may depend as much on your playing style as on personal preference. Many players think a highly curved fingerboard feels comfortable, especially when playing chords. A flat fingerboard, on the other hand, allows for high-note string bends without choking the strings to the frets higher up the neck.

Compound radius

A *compound radius* fingerboard becomes flatter toward the body. For example, it goes from 9.5" at the nut (for comfortable chord fingering) to 15" at the body (for choke-free high-register string bends).

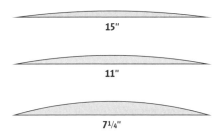

15"

11"

7¹/₄"

The radius tells you how flat or rounded the fingerboard is (actual dimensions shown).

Wood

Maple and mahogany are commonly used materials for guitar necks. Maple necks typically make for a brighter, more transparent type of sound. Mahogany tends to enhance a warmer tone with a stronger midrange. It's hard to judge the quality of a neck, but it should have a straight, even grain along its entire length. Necks can be made of one solid block, or built up of several pieces (and types) of wood.

Fingerboard

Rosewood and maple are the two most commonly used woods for the fingerboard. Rosewood fingerboards, with a dark brown hue, help produce a warm sound with an accented midrange, typically loved by rock players. Maple fingerboards are often one with the neck, rather than being a separate, glued-on piece of wood. They're blonde and lacquered, and make for a brighter, punchier tone with more bite and attack. Ebony, a nearly black, extremely hard type of wood, is used mainly on expensive basses.

Bright or warm?
Of course, the type of wood used for the fingerboard is just one of the many elements that make for the sound of an instrument. This helps explain why some describe the effect of a pau ferro fingerboard as 'bright,' while others say 'warm.'

Composite
A few brands use either composite (phenol) fingerboards, which have a very smooth, 'plastic' feel, or phenolic-impregnated wooden fingerboards. The latter, also known as Pheno-wood fingerboards, are harder and more durable than pure wood, and they have a more natural feel and a better tone than phenol.

Dots, stars, stripes...
Usually, the position markers or *fingerboard markers* are simple dot inlays. There are plenty of other shapes available though, ranging from stars and blocks to bow ties, dice, and thunderbolts. No matter what they're made of (abalone, shell, or mother-of-pearl; pearloid; other materials), they do not affect the sound of the instrument.

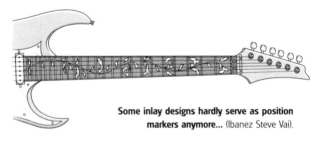

Some inlay designs hardly serve as position markers anymore... (Ibanez Steve Vai).

Set-in or bolt-on?
Necks can be glued or bolted onto the body. Most players find that instruments with *bolt-on* necks sound brighter and punchier, with a stronger and more percussive attack, and with less sustain than the ones with glued *set-in necks*. However, some of these differences can also be due to the thicker type of body that most instruments with set-in necks have.

Through-neck

A *through-neck* is a neck that runs all the way from the headstock to the tail of the instrument. This *neck-through body* or *full-length neck* design is said to enhance the instrument's sustain. It's more commonly found on basses than on guitars.

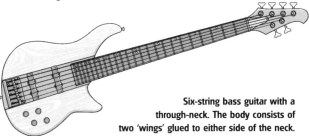

Six-string bass guitar with a through-neck. The body consists of two 'wings' glued to either side of the neck.

Truss rod slot

On instruments with a one-piece neck and fingerboard, the adjustable truss rod is inserted from the back. A dark strip of wood, visible at the back of the neck, covers the slot.

From the side

Most truss rods have their adjustment nut either at the headstock (hidden under a small cover), or at the other end of the neck. In the latter case, you may have to remove the pickguard to get to it. Also, there are truss rods that can be conveniently adjusted from the side of the neck. A warning: Neck adjustments are best left to a guitar technician.

Dual action

Typically, the truss rod is used to prevent the neck from getting too concave as a result of the strings' tension. A *dual-action* or *two-way* truss rod also allows the neck to be adjusted the other way around, making it a bit more concave than it was. Installing higher-tension (heavier-gauge) strings has the same effect, but this may not be what you want.

Graphite rods, carbon fiber spines

Some bass guitars and thin-neck guitars have rigid carbon fiber (graphite) rods to reinforce the neck, next to a truss rod. Other neck designs have a stiff, graphite core surrounded by feel- and sound-enhancing wood; the truss rod is located in a slot in this core. A third type of neck is made of graphite only.

One or both

There are two basic headstock designs. One has all tuning machines in line on one side. The other positions them on both sides of the headstock.

In line

With the tuning machines in line, the thin (treble) strings have to travel quite a few inches between the nut and their tuning machines. This can cause tuning instability when bending these strings or using a tremolo, unless you have either an ultra smooth nut or a *locking nut* (see page 50). Also, the extra string length requires a slightly higher string tension. This makes the string harder to bend and more prone to breakage.

Reverse headstock

If this bothers you, consider trying a neck with a *reverse headstock*. This makes the instrument look like a right-handed guitar with a left-handed neck. As a result of reversing the headstock, the string section between the nut and the tuning machines is reduced for the treble strings (making them easier to bend and less susceptible to detuning), and increased for the bass strings (making them sound tighter).

Tilted headstock

Many guitar and bass designs feature a *tilted headstock* – a headstock that is tilted slightly backward, usually at an

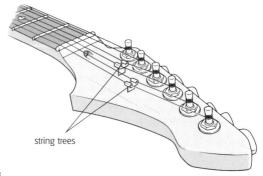

string trees

angle of 14°. This makes for a downward string tension at the nut, so that the strings don't pop out or buzz. Other designs require *string trees* or *string guides* for this purpose. However, these small metal guides may compromise your sound, sustain, and tuning stability (see page 50). As an alternative, you can use staggered tuning machines (see page 46).

Check the neck

On new instruments, if the neck and fingerboard don't feel as smooth as they should, they need to be broken in. Always check to see if the neck is straight: It shouldn't point left or right, or be warped or twisted.

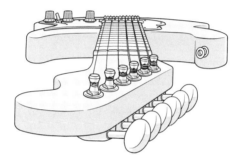

From this angle you can check whether a neck is warped or twisted.

Close to the edge

Also check whether the strings are spaced evenly across the neck. The illustration below shows a guitar with a slightly dislocated bridge. As a result, low E is so close to the edge that you keep pushing it off of the neck when playing the higher frets.

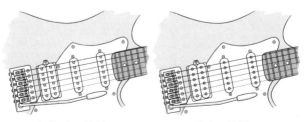

badly-placed bridge   well-placed bridge

On the guitar on the left, the low E-string is too close to the edge of the neck.

Dead spots

The fingerboard must be smooth and free from knots, cracks, and chips. Play each string in all positions, listening carefully for *dead spots* – positions where the note suddenly drops off or sounds much softer. Do so both amplified and acoustically. However, some players are convinced that dead spots – to a certain extent – are pretty much unavoidable in great sounding instruments, stating that instruments without them usually sound consistently shallow and have little 'character.'

THE SCALE

Both guitars and basses come with different string lengths, known as the *scale*.

Range

Instruments with a longer scale tend to sound slightly fuller or warmer, with a bit of extra sustain, while instruments with shorter strings allow for easier fingering and faster licks. Also, on long-scale necks strings need to be bent further to get the required pitch.

Guitar scales

Most guitar scales are between 24" and 25.5" (62–65 cm). If you like much-lower-than-standard tunings, an instrument with an extra-long scale will help prevent flopping strings (see page 119).

Children

To enable young beginners to play the instrument, some companies make *¾ guitars*, with scales that are about three to four inches shorter. Some players use these down-sized models as *travel guitars*.

Basses

Basses have much longer scales than guitars. They range from 30" to 36". Most bassists go for a *long-scale* model (34"). Some players, including pros, prefer a medium scale, which is more comfortable to play, especially if you have smaller hands. *Short-scale basses* (30") are mainly used by children. Compared to the larger sizes, they tend to sound mellow, lacking a punchy low-end.

Extra-long

Super-long or extra-long scales (35"–36") are mainly used for five- and six-string basses, which have an extra low B-string. The extra length results in a higher string tension, which promotes the definition of low B, as well as focus and sustain. However, super-long scales do require large hands or flexible fingers – or both. Also, the extra tension can make the G-string sound a bit nasal.

Speaking length

The scale is known also as the *vibrating* or *speaking length* of the strings. However, the string sections between the nut and the tuning machines also vibrate – and therefore they influence the sound too (see Reverse headstock, page 38, and String changes, page 51).

Scale

The correct way to determine the scale of an instrument is to double the distance from the nut to the center of the twelfth fret. Measuring string length from the nut to the saddles isn't very exact, as the saddles may be in a different position per string.

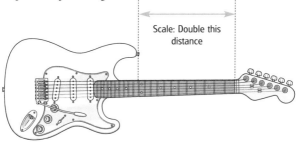

Scale: Double this distance

The scale: Double the distance from the nut to the twelfth fret.

FRETS

Most solidbodies have 21, 22, or 24 frets. The more frets, the larger your pitch range, of course. Still, many guitarists prefer instruments with 21 or 22 frets. Why? Because this design allows placement of the neck pickup exactly on the second-octave spot. On a 24-fret guitar, that's where the 24th fret is. Having 24 frets means that the neck pickup needs be moved toward the bridge, rendering its sound less warm.

Basses

The number of frets on basses ranges from 20 on most traditional designs, to 24 or even 26 on other instruments.

Frets and sound

Frets come in different sizes and shapes. String bends are easiest on large, jumbo-type frets, seen usually on the type of guitars that are built for high-speed solos and lots of volume: 24 frets, a shallow neck, a flat fingerboard, a Floyd Rose-type tremolo, and humbuckers in the bridge and neck positions. Conversely, smaller (vintage) frets facilitate chord playing, as well as sliding along the neck.

Shape

The shape of the frets has a minor impact on the sound. Broader designs tend to make for a slightly broader tone, and edgier frets for a slightly edgier tone.

Zero fret

Some guitars and basses have a *zero fret*, right next to the nut. As a result, all strings always run over a fret – whether fretted or not – so open strings have the same timbre as fretted strings.

Check

Always check to see that there are no frets sticking out of the neck (making playing painful), and make sure the frets are long enough to prevent your E-strings from slipping off of the neck. Also, the frets should be leveled to prevent strings from buzzing of choking against them, and they should be properly rounded and polished to make for a smooth feel and easy string bends. Badly fitted or poorly finished frets can cause dead spots and buzzes.

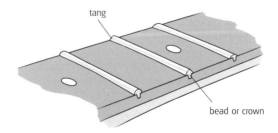

Frets come in different sizes and shapes.

Nickel silver

Most frets are made of nickel silver, a hard alloy. However, fretting will eventually cause small dents in the frets that catch the strings and hinder string bending, and frequent bending will result in flat spots. Worn frets can be milled (*i.e.*, leveled and recrowned) a couple of times by your guitar tech, until it's time to replace them.

Fretless basses and guitars

Tipcode EGTR-006

Many bassists prefer the sound of a *fretless bass*. Eliminating the metal frets gives these instruments a hard-to-describe, mellow, singing tone, a less percussive attack, and a characteristic sustain. It also makes playing in tune quite a bit harder: On a fretless instrument, the exact pitch of a note isn't determined by a fret, but by where exactly you put your finger on the fingerboard. Even the smallest deviation makes you sound out of tune. Fretless guitars are rare, but they do exist.

Stripes

To help you play in tune, some fretless basses have thin, inlaid stripes instead of frets. These strips show you where to put your fingers. The lesser the contrast between the stripes and the fingerboard, the less visible they are, both for you and the audience.

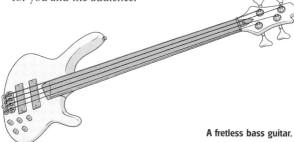

A fretless bass guitar.

Take them out

Rather then buying a fretless instrument, you can have the frets of a fretted one replaced by inlaid stripes. The main disadvantage of this procedure is that you can't tell what the bass will sound like in advance. You can have it refretted again if you don't like the result, of course – but searching a readily-made fretless instrument may be less troublesome, and much cheaper.

More and different frets

To compensate for tuning deviations (see page 102), or for other purposes that go beyond the scope of this Tipbook, some instruments come with different fret configurations or fret shapes, ranging from curved frets to combinations of short and long

TUNING MACHINES

Good tuning machines are mainly important for ease and stability of tuning – but there's more to them than just that.

Enclosed machines

Almost all guitars have enclosed tuning machines with sealed metal housings. Such machines don't need additional lubrication. Non-sealed housings usually have a small opening that you can use to apply oil.

Open back

Tuning machines with an open back are used mostly on bass guitars and some types of vintage guitars. They're more susceptible to dust and dirt, which is no problem as long as you keep them clean and (sparsely) lubricated.

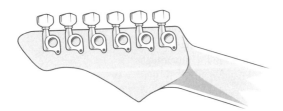

Sealed tuning machine; the standard on guitars.

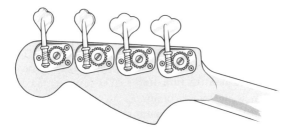

Many basses have open tuning machines.

Adjustable tension

On some types of tuning machines the tension can be adjusted with the small screw on top of the button. Turning the screw makes the machine go tighter or looser.

Slotted machines

Most basses and some guitars have *slotted* or *split-shaft* tuning machines, with the hole for the string running lengthwise through the tuning post (or *shaft*). This cleans up the look as the string ends are hidden in the tuning posts. Also, slotted shaft tuners make fitting strings easier. On the other hand, they require that the strings be cut to length before they are fit. This can be awkward if one breaks during a gig. A tip: You can of course pre-cut spare strings.

Locking machines

Fitting new strings is easiest with *locking tuning machines.* Some of these designs have a special thumbscrew to lock the string. Others have a built-in, self-actuated locking mechanism. The main advantage of locking machines is that the strings don't need to be wrapped around the tuning posts. This enhances tuning stability (see page 84).

Finer control

The *gear ratio* of a tuning machine indicates how many times you need to turn the button to make the tuning post go round once. The higher the gear ratio, the finer the control it provides. Most

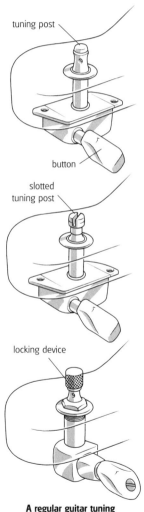

tuning post

button

slotted
tuning post

locking device

A regular guitar tuning
machine, a slotted ('vintage')
design, and a locking machine.

guitar tuning machines are 12:1, 14:1, or 16:1. Bass tuning machines typically range from 20:1 to 28:1.

Staggered tuning machines

To eliminate the need for string trees, which may negatively affect your instrument's sound, sustain, and tuning stability (see page 50), some guitars have *staggered tuning machines*: The tuning posts get shorter as the strings get thinner. This pulls the thin strings down, increasing their pressure on the nut – just like string trees or tilted headstocks do.

New machines

Replacing budget or worn machines with good new ones will make tuning easier and help improve tuning stability. A set of good tuning machines, made to high tolerances and using good materials, typically costs forty to sixty dollars or more.

Checking out machines

The strings' pitches should change at the slightest turn of the machine head buttons. If they don't, there may be play in the tuning machines – especially if it's an old or a cheap instrument. A tip: If a string binds in its slot in the nut, it won't immediately respond to the tuning machine either (see page 102).

THE BRIDGE

The bridge is the part where the strings connect to the body. The strings can be attached to the bridge itself, or to a separate tailpiece.

Tremolo or fixed

Tremolo guitars have either a *tremolo bridge* (as opposed to a *fixed bridge*) or a *tremolo tailpiece*. Both are dealt with on page 49 and onward. Non-tremolo instruments are sometimes referred to as *hard-tail* guitars.

Heavy

A bridge can be anything from a basic, bent piece of steel to a heavy, solid brass affair. The latter will help make for a fuller sound and added sustain. Some basses come with individual bridges per string.

String-through-body bridges

The term *string-through-body (STB) bridge* is self-explanatory. This design increases the string-to-body contact, which slightly boosts the effect that the body wood has on the sound. Also, a string-through-body bridge tends to make the sound a bit brighter, tighter (important for low B on a five-string bass!), or snappier. This is a result of the slightly increased string length and the smaller string angle over the bridge saddles. Some say that STB-bridges enhance sustain as well.

Convertible bridges

A few instruments have a convertible bridge, which lets you either 'top-load' the strings, or attach them through the body.

Tailpieces

A tailpiece that is fixed to the top of the instrument, rather than to its tail, is commonly known as a *stop tailpiece* or *stopbar tailpiece*. Confusingly, both terms are also used to indicate bridge designs that double as tailpieces.

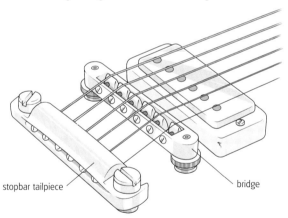

stopbar tailpiece

bridge

Adjustments

Most guitars bridges have individual string saddles: Each string runs over a saddle, which can be adjusted in one, two, or three ways.

- The saddles can be moved lengthwise to adjust intonation (see page 109).
- Lowering or raising the saddles alters the action or string height. If there are no separate saddles, the entire bridge can be raised or lowered.

• A three-dimensional adjustment allows you to adjust string spacing as well. This is usually seen on basses only.

Bass string spacing

On basses, a ⅝" (16 mm) spacing is considered narrow; a spacing of ¾" (19 mm) and up is wide. Most slapping bassists prefer a wider string spacing than finger-style players do. Basses with wider string spacing usually have wider necks too – and wider necks tend to slow down string crossings.

Saddles

The saddles are often stainless steel affairs. The extra mass of big, brass saddles is said to enhance output, tone, and sustain. Some companies make synthetic saddles that increase both the instrument's sound and the strings' life expectancy.

Floating bridge and tailpiece

Like violins, hollow-body guitars usually have a wooden, one-piece *floating bridge* that is kept in place by the strings' tension. Intonation and string height can be adjusted to a limited extent only. The *floating tailpiece*, often a prominent design in metal or wood, is attached to an interior block at the tail of the soundbox.

Floating pickup

Some – expensive – hollowbodies have a *floating pickup* as well. A floating pickup is attached to the pickguard, rather

A floating bridge, a floating wooden tailpiece, and a floating pickup (Elferink).

than to the instrument's top. This allows the top to vibrate freely.

TREMOLO

Tipcode EGTR-003

Basically, all tremolos work alike. They allow you to change the tension and thus the pitch of all strings simultaneously, using an arm that is attached to a moveable bridge or tailpiece.

Pitch bend and vibrato

Technically speaking, this effect is not a tremolo: 'Sliding' from one pitch to another is referred to as a *pitch bend*, and small, fast pitch variations are known as *vibrato*. Still, 'tremolo' is the most popular term for this system. *Trem, vibrato unit*, and *whammy* are some of the alternative names.

Synchronized tremolo

The best-known tremolo system probably is the one found on the original Fender Stratocaster and many of the guitars based on that design. It's known as a *synchronized tremolo*, and it can be set up in two ways. One is with the bridge's base plate resting on the body; this allows the player to only lower string tension. More commonly, the bridge is set up so that you can also raise the strings' pitches. In this case, the bridge's base plate floats a bit above the instrument's top.

Basic, synchronized tremolo.

Bigsby

Another system, the Bigsby *vibrato unit*, features a large handle and a fixed bridge. The string tension is altered with a moving tailpiece. Guitars with this type of vibrato are used mainly in country and 1960s-style guitar bands.

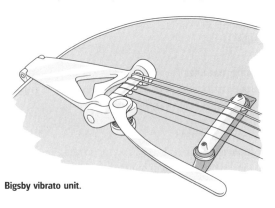

Bigsby vibrato unit.

Detuning strings

Tremolos (and string bends) can cause severe tuning problems. How? When the trem arm is released, the strings may not return to their original pitch due to friction at the nut, the string trees, or the saddles. Also, using the tremolo will vary the tension on the string wraps around the tuning posts (see page 84). Another culprit? The strings' ball ends, which move back and forth in the bridge when using the tremolo, may not have returned to their original positions. A *double-locking tremolo* is the answer to these problems.

Floyd Rose

The best-known double locking tremolo bears the name of its designer, Floyd Rose. Apart from allowing for impressive pitch variations, both up and down, it features two locking systems. At the bridge, the strings are locked with small clamps, rather than using ball ends. At the other end, they're anchored by a *locking nut*.

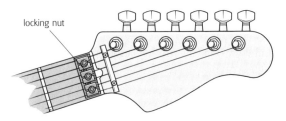

locking nut

A locking nut clamps the strings at the nut.

Clamp

A locking nut clamps the strings down at the nut, so that using the tremolo won't affect the exact position of the wraps around the tuning posts – and thus the tuning – anymore.

Fine-tuning machines

Of course, a locking nut renders the regular tuning machines useless. That's why guitars with a locking nut have *fine-tuning machines* or *fine tuners* at the bridge.

String changes

A locking nut makes changing strings a bit harder: You need tools for both the locking nut and the bridge clamps, and you need to cut the strings' ball ends before you can fit them. A locking nut also influences the sound, as the string sections behind the nut are cut off. With a regular nut, these sections will also vibrate.

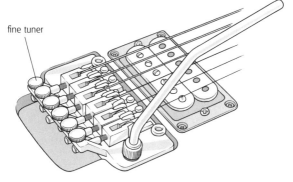

fine tuner

Floyd Rose tremolo system with bridge and fine-tuning machines (Jackson).

Dive bombing

Floyd Rose tremolos and similar designs can be found on many guitars for players who like musical dive bombing, fast and loud solos, and severe string bendings. This type of guitar usually features 24 large frets, one or more humbuckers, and a narrow, relatively flat neck with a slim (C-type) profile.

Different solutions

Rather than lock the strings at the bridge and the nut, some guitar makers prefer to make them slide more smoothly at those points, for instance by using special nuts (page 53), or string ends (bullets, rather than balls) or by getting rid of the string trees (page 46). Special *locking* tuning machines can help prevent detuning strings by reducing or eliminating the number of wraps at the tuning posts (page 45).

Detuning
When checking out new tremolo guitars, you'll find that the strings detune quickly because they haven't stabilized yet. Also, note that when you play string bends on tremolo guitars, the pitch of the adjacent strings will change too (a result of the bent string pulling the bridge up a little). On guitars with fixed bridges, they won't.

The arm
Tremolo arms come in screw-in, pop-in, bayonet, and other versions. Some are designed to stay at your fingertips all the time. Others drop down as soon as you let go, and there are arms that can be adjusted to do either. Pop-in arms are the easiest ones to remove or attach. If their receiver is not adjustable, these arms may at one point start falling out of the trem block themselves.

U-bar
If you like a trem, but don't like its arm, it's good to know that some types of tremolo can be operated – to a limited extent – with your palm. Other designs feature a U-bar instead of the traditional arm.

Less sustain?
Some experts believe that tremolo systems reduce the instrument's sustain, as the springs absorb some of the vibrations – but there are plenty of tremolo guitars with great sustain.

Breaking strings and tremolos
If a spring breaks on a tremolo guitar, the tremolo springs will make the other strings go up in pitch. In other words, you can't finish the song without retuning your instrument or replacing the broken string.

Locking your tremolo
The term *locking tremolo* is also used for tremolos that can

be locked to make them behave like a fixed, hard-tail bridge. If you want to be able to lock your tremolo temporarily, some companies make little devices that simply secure the trem's arm.

NUTS

Most nuts are made of plastic or metal. Hollowbody players often prefer organic materials, such as bone or fossil ivory. Metal nuts reduce the tonal difference between open and fretted strings (unless you have a zero fret), and may add a little extra brightness to the sound. Heavy metal nuts will also increase the sustain. Plastic nuts can help remove unwanted twang from your tone, and decrease the effect of buzzing strings, but they're most likely to cause friction.

Smooth

The harder and smoother a nut is, the easier tuning will be. A hard, smooth nut will also improve tuning stability: If you bend strings or use your tremolo, the strings have to be able to move through the slots without binding. High quality synthetic, carbon, or graphite nuts have been specifically designed for these purposes. Also, there are nuts with built-in rollers and ball bearings.

Slots

When switching to heavier-gauge strings, the nut's slots should be wide enough to keep them from getting stuck. If the slots are too wide, though, strings may buzz in them.

Adjustable nuts

To adjust string height, nuts can be lowered (with a file), raised (with shims), or replaced – all jobs for a professional. Only few instruments come with a height-adjustable nut.

PICKUPS

The sound of a (bass) guitar depends a great deal on the pickups. After all, these are the devices that convert the notes you play to the electric signals that are eventually turned into sound. This section deals with the main characteristics of the various types of pickup, without getting too technical.

Bridge and neck   Tipcode EGTR-007

Most guitars have two or three pickups: a bridge or *rear pickup*, a neck or *front pickup*, and often one in the middle too. Even if they're all the same, each will generate a different sound – just like hitting the strings in these various places does. Most basses have one or two pickups.

Treble and rhythm

Typically, the bridge pickup will produce a brighter, edgier, treblier, twangier, more aggressive type of sound, similar to what happens if you play the strings closer to the bridge. Playing closer to the neck has a similar effect to using the neck pickup. In other words: Using the neck pickup makes for a smoother, cleaner, warmer timbre. Some pickup selectors are labeled 'treble' and 'rhythm' to indicate the bridge and neck pickups respectively.

A coil and a magnet

Simply put, a pickup is a magnet with a length of thin copper wire wound around it thousands of times – the *coil*. When you play, the vibrating strings cause changes in the magnetic field that surrounds the magnet. The pickup converts these changes into electric signals that are sent to the amp.

Humbuckers

Unfortunately, pickups also pick up unwanted signals – hum and noise, as you can clearly hear when you turn up

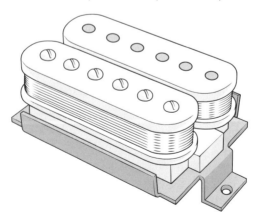

A humbucker with individually adjustable pole pieces (see page 65).

the volume on some guitars. The solution, devised in 1955, was to make a pickup with two coils. The way these two coils are set up (for technicians: reverse polarity, reverse winding) makes them buck the hum. Their common name is taken from this pleasant feature: They're called *humbuckers*.

A different sound
Tipcode EGTR-008

Humbuckers sound quite different from *single-coil pickups*: fatter, beefier, meatier, warmer, broader. This is in part because they have a broader magnetic field, and in part because they don't cancel hum only, but a bit of brightness as well. *Mini-humbuckers*, with a narrower magnetic field, produce a brighter, more open tone.

Single-coil pickups
The sound of single-coil pickups is typically described as clear, bright, tight, clean, cool, snappy, twangy, or glassy, with more bite and attack.

Dummy coil
If you want the sound, but not the hum of a single-coil pickup, you can get pickups with an extra 'dummy' coil. This extra coil is meant to just buck the hum without influencing the bright sound of the main coil. Some of these noiseless *stacked pickups*, *stacks*, or *vertical humbuckers* tend to be a bit less dynamic, though.

Pickup layouts
Many guitars have humbucking or single-coil pickups only; others feature a combination of the two. Pickup layouts

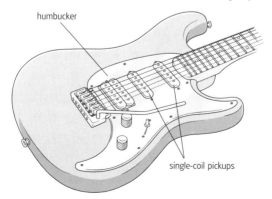

humbucker

single-coil pickups

are often referred to by single letter combinations. For example, HSS means that the guitar has a humbucker at the bridge, followed by single-coil pickups in the middle and neck positions.

Single-coil or humbucker?

Both single-coil and humbucking pickups are available in many different versions, and both types of pickup can be used in pretty much any style of music. The choice depends on taste, mainly, and on what you're playing. For example, with an HSS configuration you can use the humbucker for a scorching, heavily distorted solo, the middle pickup for a clean ballad, and the neck pickup for some smooth

Gibson Les Paul®

Fender Stratocaster®

Two very well-known solid-body designs: one with two humbuckers, the other with three single-coil pickups.

chords. Two general rules are that 1) almost all jazz guitars have two humbuckers, and 2) the type of guitar with a Floyd Rose tremolo and a 24-fret neck often has an HSH pickup configuration.

Coil-taps and humbucking singles

On some guitars, one or both humbuckers can be used as single coils as well, so you can have the best of both worlds. A special switch (*coil-tap* or *coil-splitter*) simply disables one of the two coils of the humbucker. Likewise, two single-coil pickups can be wired so that they behave and sound like a humbucker.

Bass pickups

Most of what has been said above goes for bass pickups too. However, single-coil pickups do not present so much of a humming problem on basses.

J or P

Many bass pickups are modeled after Fender's Jazz Bass and Precision Bass pickups. Because these are registered trademarks, the pickups of other brands are often labeled J-style and P-style, for example. The P-style pickup is a very recognizable split-coil humbucking design. It's mounted in middle pickup position (basses don't have pickups close to the neck) and provides a low, thick, rocky sound. On basses, bridge pickups produce more of a midrange, growling type of sound.

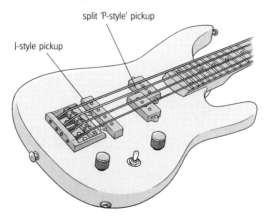

split 'P-style' pickup

J-style pickup

Two popular types of bass pickups.

TONE AND VOLUME

Most guitars and basses have very plain, basic tone and volume controls. They must be well-placed, feel smooth and solid, and work evenly throughout their entire rotation.

How many

Some players prefer an instrument with just one shared volume control and one shared tone control for all pickups; others like more options. If you have a volume control for each pickup, you can blend their sounds rather than just choose one or the other. Likewise, having a tone control for each pickup allows you to create different sounds, and to change from one to the other by using the pickup selector only.

Tone control

Tone controls on guitars and basses are usually *treble cut* models. When they're fully open, the sound is at its brightest. Turning them counterclockwise will cut the higher (treble) frequencies, gradually making the sound darker or thicker.

Volume control

On many instruments, the volume control affects the tone as well: If you reduce the volume, the treble is cut too, to some extent. This is one reason why many (bass)guitarists play-test their instruments with all controls wide open – so they can hear everything there is. The treble-cut effect of a volume control can sometimes be eliminated by having your guitar technician install a capacitor.

More controls

There are many more types of controls available, ranging from five-step frequency range switches to active midrange boosters, or the possibility to switch between using more or less windings of a pickup (*tapped pickup*), for example. Instruments with an active EQ (see page 61) offer additional tone control too.

Balance control

Rather than a pickup selector, most basses have a balance control that allows you to choose one pickup or the other, or a blend of both. Alternatively, they have a volume control for each pickup. Balance controls often have a center detent, so you can 'feel' the middle position.

Potentiometer
The technical term for the devices that are controlled with the volume or tone knobs is *potentiometer* or *pot*.

Output jack
The signal from the pickup(s) leaves your instrument at the output jack. As this is where you plug *in* your cable, it is often – mistakenly – referred to as an *input*. A tip: Worn output jacks can be a source of noise. They can be easily replaced.

PICKUP SELECTORS
The pickup selector or toggle switch allows you to choose which pickup(s) you use – but there's more.

Three-way
Most guitars with two pickups have a three-way *toggle switch*, allowing you to choose either the bridge pickup (position 1), both pickups (2), or the neck pickup (3).

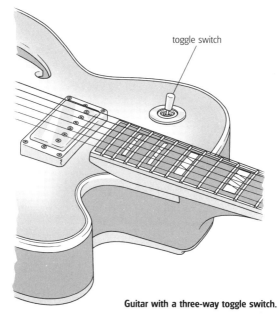

toggle switch

Guitar with a three-way toggle switch.

Five-way

If your guitar has three pickups, it'll usually have a five-way selector: bridge pickup (position 1), bridge and middle pickups (position 2), middle (3), middle and neck (4), neck pickup (5).

Humbucking single-coils

On some guitars, the selector has a position that makes two single-coil pickups behave like a humbucker. (For technicians: This requires the middle pickup to have reverse winding and reverse polarity.)

In series or in parallel

Usually, the two coils of a humbucker are connected *in series*. On some guitars you can use humbuckers *in parallel* too, with a flick of the pickup selector. Without getting too technical, this means that they start behaving like single coils, with a glassier, brighter, clearer sound, and a reduced output.

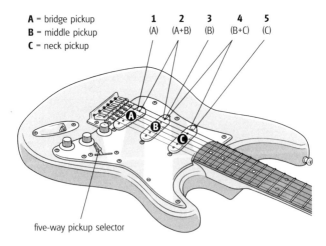

A = bridge pickup
B = middle pickup
C = neck pickup

1	2	3	4	5
(A)	(A+B)	(B)	(B+C)	(C)

five-way pickup selector

This is how a regular five-way pickup selector works.

Out of phase

The two coils of a humbucker are traditionally wired *in phase*. On some guitars, the pickup selector offers an *out of phase* setting too. This makes for a thin, frail sound with little output that's often severely boosted, or used for specific effects.

Solo? Direct out!

For solos, most players use the bridge pickup, and tone and volume controls are wide open. A *direct-out switch* gets you there immediately. It sends the bridge pickup's signal directly to the amp, and bypasses tone and volume controls (so they behave like they're open).

BASSES WITH ACTIVE EQUALIZERS

Basses with an *active EQ* (*equalizer*) or *active preamplifier* have extended tone controls. These allow you to not only *cut* bass, mid, or treble frequencies, but to *boost* them as well.

Parametric

Apart from this *three-band* control, you can usually choose the exact midrange frequency you want to cut or boost. This is known as a *swept* or *parametric mid EQ.*

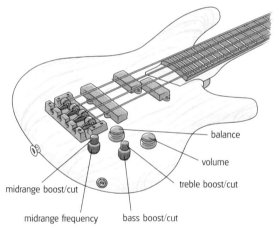

balance

volume

midrange boost/cut

treble boost/cut

midrange frequency   bass boost/cut

An active EQ provides additional tonal variation. Stacked knobs save space.

Less noise, more output

Basses with active electronics can be used with long cables without any loss in sound or dynamics (see page 87). To cope with the enhanced output of the active preamp, most bass amplifiers have a separate 'active' input.

Battery

The active preamplifier is usually powered by one or two 9-volt batteries. These can last up to two or three thousand playing hours, provided you don't forget to unplug your instrument cable when you're done playing. (This turns the preamp off.)

Active or passive?

Active basses are often said to sound tighter, cleaner, and more focused, but less organic, warm, or lively than passive basses. That said, many active basses have a switch that turns them into passive instruments. A warning: Active basses that do not offer that option can't do without a battery!

Optional

On some basses an active EQ is an option, usually costing some one to two hundred dollars extra.

MORE PICKUPS

There are many more types of pickups than the ones described above. Here are some examples.

Active pickups

Both guitars and basses can be provided with active pickups, which have a weaker type of magnet and less windings than passive pickups. The resulting lower output is boosted by a built-in preamp.

Active pickups provide a clean, noise-free, and very even signal, which works great with multi-effect devices, or for players who want a heavily distorted sound without losing definition or clarity, and without feedback. Also, string pull (page 64) is never a problem. Advocates of passive pickups, however, often claim that active pickups sound a bit too clean, and lack dynamics.

Expensive

Passive pickups are still the industry standard. In part, this is due to the price of active pickups. A set costs well over two hundred dollars. A note: Most *active* bass guitars also have *passive* pickups. These basses are called 'active' because of their active preamp and EQ.

Piezo pickups

Some basses and a few guitars have additional non-magnetic *piezo pickups* (see page 121). These pickups are similar to the ones used on electric-acoustic guitars. On electric guitars, they generate a bright, clear, 'acoustic' type of sound. On basses, they're said to help produce a big, deep sound with lots of bright definition, which is generally more useful for solos and chordal playing than for regular bass parts.

Invisible

Piezo pickups are usually built invisibly into the bridge. To get a balanced sound, the gain can be adjusted per string, using one pickup for each string and individual *trim pots* in one of the body cavities. On some instruments, the balance between the piezo and the magnetic pickups can be set too. Others have dual outputs – one for the each type of pickup, so you can choose to use different types of amps too.

And furthermore...

… there are special pickups that allow for infinite sustain; and pickups with no less than four coils; and pickups that use infrared light beams rather than magnets; and much more…

MORE ABOUT PICKUPS

Knowing a little more about pickups can make it easier to find the guitar or bass of your choice, and to choose replacement pickups for your instrument.

Windings

Pickups vary in tone and output as a result of numerous variables. One of the most obvious parameters is the number of windings. More windings make for a 'hotter pickup' with a higher output; more mids and less treble; and a warmer, darker (but less clear or transparent) tone. The hotter a pickup, the easier it will be to create overdriven sounds and infinite sustain. Solo guitarists typically prefer hot pickups; chords often sound better using lower output pickups.

Type of magnet

Many catalogs specify the type of magnet for each pickup. The most common types are Alnico 2 (II), Alnico 5 (V), and ceramic magnets. Alnico 2 is often said to promote a warm, dark tone. Alnico 5 is frequently used for pickups that are designed for a brighter sound and a higher output. Ceramic magnets help contribute to a very transparent, snappier, brighter (if you like it) or edgier, harsher (if you don't) sound with a strong attack.

Immaterial

However, there are experts who claim that magnet material isn't that crucial at all. After all, there are very warm sounding ceramic pickups…

Pickups and prices

Budget instruments often lack expressiveness and tonal richness, which can be due to the use of cheaper (ceramic, ferrite, or other non-Alnico) pickups. Some guitars in the two-hundred-dollar price range do come with Alnico pickups, though. Likewise, some professional instruments have ceramic pickups for an aggressive, in-your-face tone.

String pull

If a pickup with a strong magnet is too close to the strings, it may actually pull on them. This phenomenon, *string pull*, can cause anything from undesirable overtones to rattling strings, loss of sustain, and out-of-tune notes. The common solution is to adjust the pickup a bit farther away from the strings (see page 114). Guitars with *high-impedance* pickups are more sensitive to string pull than instruments with (usually active) *low-impedance* pickups.

Single bar or individual pole pieces

Most pickups have as many *pole pieces* as they have strings. When you bend your strings, the signal may decrease as the strings are pushed toward the 'dead spots' between the pole pieces. Using pickups with a single magnetic *bar* or

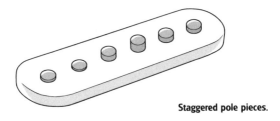

Staggered pole pieces.

blade solves this problem. Bar pickups typically produce a less percussive attack and a stronger sustain.

Adjustable, staggered, or flat
There are pickup designs that allow you to adjust the height of each pole piece for a balanced output per string. Also, there are pickups available with either *level* or *staggered pole pieces* – and there are guitars that offer a choice between the two.

The difference
If you replace a flat-pole pickup by a staggered design, the result will be a slightly different tonal balance from string to string. Generally speaking, though, staggered-magnet pickups work better with guitars with arched (low radius) fingerboards, while flat-pole designs tend to yield better results when used on instruments with modern, flatter, high-radius fingerboards.

Soaked in wax
When you play loud, pickups can act like microphones and produce feedback. To prevent this, good pickups are soaked in a potting solution (*e.g.*, wax).

Pickup covers
Pickups often have nicknames based on the looks of their protective covers. *Lipstick pickups* have a (fake) lipstick tube cover, and a *soapbar pickup* has a broad rectangular cover.

Metal, plastic, nothing
Metal covers influence the magnetic field, of course, unlike plastic pickup covers. If you'd have two identical pickups, one with a metal cover, the other with a plastic (or no) cover, the first would sound a bit less bright, and have a somewhat smaller dynamic range. A warning: Leave removing or replacing pickup covers to a technician.

Right angle or offset
Many instruments have the bridge pickup not at a right angle to the strings, but slightly offset. This makes the treble strings sound a bit brighter, with a little extra bite: Having their pole pieces closer to the bridge makes them sound as if you were playing them closer to the bridge.

Guitars and synthesizers

Electric guitars and basses can be linked to synthesizers, sequencers, and other electronic equipment. This requires a special type of pickup, often referred to as a *divider pickup*, *MIDI pickup*, or *hex pickup*. The pickup sends its signals either directly to a dedicated guitar synthesizer, or to a converter that can be hooked up to the huge variety of electronic instruments and equipment that features *MIDI* (Musical Instrument Digital Interface).

REPLACING PICKUPS

Most guitarists and bassists would rather buy another instrument than replace their pickups – but it can't hurt to consider the second option as a cost-effective way to improve your sound. Prices of good aftermarket pickups range from some fifty to a hundred dollars and more.

Try them out

The problem in choosing pickups is that you can't just try them out on your own instrument. Instead, you have to rely on your salesperson's advice and on the description pickup makers supply you with in their catalogs. A few companies present all their pickups on CD – but then you still don't know how they sound in *your* instrument and with *your* amp.

Technical data

Some catalogs have loads of technical data that may help you choose a pickup. For example, a higher *DC resistance* can indicate a higher output and a fatter sound; the height of a pickup's *resonant peak* may tell you about its clarity of sound (higher is brighter). However, it takes quite a bit of additional knowledge and experience to translate this information into sound – and your ears will probably tell you a lot more.

Enhance or compensate

New pickups can enhance certain characteristics of your instrument, or compensate for them. For example, you can buy pickups that make your guitar sound a bit brighter or twangier. Likewise, guitar and bass makers may combine brighter sounding woods with warmer sounding pickups, for instance. Want a vintage sound? Some companies produce special pickups that help you recreate that warm, smooth timbre.

Radius and string spacing, neck or bridge

New pickups should match your instrument's design. For example, there are pickups for wider and narrower string spacings, and pickups that have been designed to match either flatter or more curved fingerboards. Some pickup designs require separate left- and right-hand versions (the pickups being dissimilar for the low- and the high-pitched strings). Others are designed for use either in neck or bridge positions only (the latter usually being stronger to make up for the smaller string movement near the bridge), or in both positions.

Rewiring

You can customize your instrument by having it rewired (to add to or change the options your pickup selector offers you, for example), or by having a volume potentiometer with a different value installed (the lower the value, the darker the sound), or by many other operations that require the use of a soldering gun and more knowledge of electronics than you'll get from this book. Some companies offer their guitars with a choice of wiring options.

PLAY-TESTING

In the end, choosing an instrument is all about playing it. Here are some pointers.

Avoid damage

First of all, avoid damaging the instruments you play-test with belt buckles, zippers, and other metal parts of your clothing.

Well-adjusted

You can judge instruments only if they're well-adjusted: action, neck, pickup height, intonation… Please refer to Chapter 10 for more information.

Pro instruments

Even if your budget is limited, it can't hurt to include

professional instruments in your quest: Knowing what great instruments sound, feel, and play like will also help you to find the best instrument for your budget.

Too many guitars
Selecting instruments gets less confusing if you don't compare too many of them at a time. So pick out three guitars or basses, based on the salesperson's advice or your own ears or eyes, and play them for a while. Then swap the one you like least for another instrument. Listen again. And so on, until you've found the one you're looking for.

Too many things
Also, don't compare too many things at a time. If, for example, you use the neck pickup most of the time, compare various instruments using the neck pickup only. Try out other options (pickups, tone settings, etc.) once you've narrowed it down to a few final instruments.

One amp
Use one amp only. If not, you're comparing amps as much as you're comparing instruments – every amplifier has its own sound. Also bring your own instrument, if you have one, so you can use it as a reference. You may even want to bring your own amp, as it is such a crucial element of your sound.

Which amp
If bringing your own amp is not an option, use a similar one. Keep from experimenting with other amps – and effects – until you've limited your choice to a few instruments. If you're buying both a guitar and an amp, it's usually wisest to start with the guitar, and then look for an amp that stresses, completes, perfects, or enhances the instrument's sound.

Clean
Consider playing all instruments 'clean' first. This tells you a lot more about their true character than using overdrive channels and effects. Likewise, it's a good idea to have all volume and tone controls fully open. If you're comparing active bass guitars, set their tone controls to their 'neutral' center detents.

No amp

Even if they're solidbodies, it's good to judge instruments acoustically as well. What a bass or guitar sounds like unamplified will tell you a lot about its character and sonic properties. Listen to the instrument's timbre, play all positions at the fingerboard and listen for sustain (and dead spots…), and listen to everything else mentioned in this chapter. If you press your ear against the body, you'll be able to hear every nuance. When you're choosing a hollow-body guitar, it's even more important to also judge it acoustically.

More and more

Once you're left with a few instruments to choose from, play them longer and try out all pickup selector settings, tone and volume controls, and anything else you need to assess their quality and sound potential.

Balance

Playing along the fingerboard and across the strings can bring out the instrument's balance in volume, timbre, and sustain. For example, the thinner strings will always sound shorter and brighter than the thicker strings, but they shouldn't sound as if they were mounted on different instruments.

Dynamics and response

Play the strings as soft as you will in performance, and see if the instrument responds immediately. Play as loud as you ever will (or as loud as the store owner allows you to), and check if the instrument holds up. Good guitars and basses have a large dynamic range (from loud to soft), unless they were designed to be played extremely loud only.

Timbre

Guitarists and bassists use thousands of words and expressions to indicate an instrument's timbre or character, and there are thousands of things you can listen for. What's important to you mainly depends on the music you want to use the instrument for, and on your personal taste, of course – a bright or a dark sound, major transparency or massive power, wet or tight highs, punchy or warm lows, a smooth or a percussive midrange…

Versatility

While many guitars and basses have been designed with a specific sound or style of music in mind, others were built to offer lots of versatility. Still, you can't always expect to find everything you want in one single bass or guitar. This is just one of the reasons why some artists use more than one instrument onstage.

Everything

Set-in necks are said to promote sustain. And yes, many guitars with set-in necks do have an impressive sustain. But these guitar designs often have thicker bodies too, and thicker necks, and they don't have a tremolo… The message: How an instrument sounds is always the combined result of all its components – so listen to the entire instrument, and not to its parts.

The same?

Finally: No two guitars or basses sound and play exactly the same, not even if they're the same make and series. So always play an instrument before you buy it, and don't accept an 'identical' one from the stockroom.

SECONDHAND

If you buy a secondhand instrument, there are quite a few things that need special attention.

- Examine the body, neck, and fingerboard for **cracks and other damage**.
- **Small cracks** in the finish (*finish checking*) can be caused by age, but also by sudden changes in air humidity. Have an expert look at the instrument.
- Check the tuning machines for **play**. They should only rotate, and not be able to move up and down or sideways. Also, even the slightest turn should alter a string's pitch (provided the string doesn't bind in its slot in the nut).
- If the tuning machines **squeak**, a tiny drop of oil may help. New machines can be fitted if necessary. A set of good machines will set you back some thirty-five dollars or more. This doesn't include having them installed.
- **Rattles and buzzes** can be the result of bad adjustment, loose string windings, loose pickguard or adjustment screws, a worn nut, worn frets…

- Check the frets for **dents and flat spots**: Worn frets can result in buzzes and out-of-tune notes. Dented frets hamper string-bending. Refretting easily costs a hundred to more than three hundred dollars.
- Check the **pickups and the pickup selector**. Hook up the instrument and press the strings down so that they touch the pickups, one by one, or use a small metal object (such as a paperclip). You should hear a click every time you hit a pickup. Check all the pickups in all selector settings.
- If **tone and volume controls** are scratchy, the pots may need to be cleaned (see page 107) or replaced. If they're just dirty, the noise should fade a little when you rotate them a few times.
- Especially when buying privately, it may pay off to have the instrument **appraised**. Vintage instruments should be checked to see if they're truly vintage all over.

DEVELOPMENTS

Though most popular guitar and bass designs have been around for decades, there will always be room for innovation. Some examples to end this chapter.

Tremolos

Roller bearings in tremolo bridges make them move more smoothly and return to pitch more accurately. Changing strings doesn't require cutting off ball ends anymore, and a breaking string doesn't make the other strings go so far out of tune that you can't finish the song.

Digital guitars

In the world's first digital guitar (Gibson, 2002), the analog signals are converted to digital signals. This system eliminates hum, and enables you to use effects and volume, pan, or EQ settings per string – distortion on some strings, a clean sound on the others…

Modeling guitars

In 2003, Line 6 became the first company to present a modeling guitar. The Variax uses advanced modeling technology to emulate the sounds of twenty-five classic electric and acoustic guitars, available at the turn of a knob.

6. GOOD STRINGS

Strings should be easy to play, sound good, and last long – preferably without being too expensive. This chapter helps you make a choice.

The thinnest guitar strings are simply thin, steel wires. The heavier strings have a steel core that is wound with a thin metal wire or ribbon.

Differences

There's not very much difference in the sound of plain strings, from brand to brand. The wound strings show much bigger differences, and the material of the wrap wire is one of the reasons why. The three most common windings are nickel-plated steel, pure nickel, and pure (stainless) steel.

Nickel-plated steel

Most guitarists use strings with a nickel-plated steel wrap. Confusingly, these are usually referred to as *nickel-wound*.

Pure nickel

Strings with a solid nickel wrap are commonly known as *pure nickel-wound*. This type of string, which was especially popular in the 1950s and 1960s, produces a warmer, richer, vintage type of sound.

Steel

Steel-wound strings sound the brightest, with a lot of cutting power. Also, steel wrap wire can be a good choice if you have very acidic perspiration (see page 79).

The core

Some string manufacturers use a hexagonal core for their wound strings to provide better grip for the winding. Others prefer the traditional round core, stating that this produces a more even, truer tone.

Heavy and light

When you buy a set of strings, you can choose between various gauges. Here are the main characteristics of light-gauge and heavy-gauge string sets.

The main differences.

Light-gauge strings	Heavy-gauge strings
'lighter,' edgier, and twangier tone	'heavier,' fatter, more solid tone
don't sustain as long	longer sustain
have less volume	have a higher output
are easier to play and to bend	make playing a bit heavier
break more easily	last longer

010

A set of guitar strings is always referred to by the gauge of the thinnest string. These gauges are given in fractions of an inch. An 010 string measures 0.010" (0.25 mm).

Which gauge?

On solid-body guitars, 009s and 010s are the most popular choice, and you can get 0095s too. As heavier-gauge strings produce more tone, many players prefer to use the heaviest strings they still feel comfortable with – which is also a matter of getting used to heavier gauges. On the other hand, some guitars really do sound better with a lighter set.

Examples of popular guitar string gauges.

Set name	1st string	6th string
Extra Light, Ultra Light	008 (0.20 mm)	038 (0.95 mm)
Light	009	042
Regular	010	046
Medium	011	052
Heavy/Jazz	012 (0.30 mm)	054 (1.4 mm)

Names and numbers

Most manufacturers use names as well as numbers to indicate the gauges of their string sets. Above are some of the commonly used names and gauges. The gauges of the sixth strings are examples: They may vary per brand or type of string, as may the gauges of the other four strings.

W = Wound

The thinner sets usually have a plain third string (G), whereas most thicker sets have a wound G. Wound third strings are usually indicated with a W (*i.e.*, 020W). Some players prefer a wound G in light-gauge sets too, as they tend to have better tone and intonation. Various brands offer light-gauge wound Gs as single strings.

Light top/heavy bottom

Some players like to combine light-gauge treble strings (making severe string bends easier) with heavier wound strings (for a fat, strong bass sound). Such light top/heavy bottom sets are readily available.

Different strings?

If you've switched from one type of string or string gauge to another, be sure to check if your instrument needs adjustment. For example, heavier-gauge strings pull harder on the neck and the tremolo springs. Switching string brands may require adjustments as well, even if you're still using the same gauge: The strings of some brands have a higher tension than equally heavy strings from another make.

Heavier gauge

Changing to heavier-gauge strings may also cause tuning problems: The heavier strings can get caught in the nut's slots. The solution is to have the slots widened or to have the nut replaced.

Thicker core

Wound strings of a certain gauge may vary in how stiff they feel from brand to brand. You can even feel this difference without putting them on your instrument. A stiffer string will probably have a thicker core, making for a higher output, a heavier action, and a better sustain than a string with a thinner core. More flexible, thin core strings are often easier to play, sound sweeter, keep their tone longer, and have better intonation. Core thickness can vary per brand and per series.

Flat or round

Most wound strings are wrapped with a round wire. Others have a flat ribbon winding. These *flat-wound* strings are mostly used by jazz players (usually 012s), but also by surf guitarists, for example. They promote a warm, mellow, rounded, subdued tone, and produce less finger noise than the brighter-sounding *round-wounds*. Their sustain is shorter, and so is their life-expectancy: The metal 'tape' wears down faster than round wrap wire does. Conversely, flat-wound strings help extend fret life.

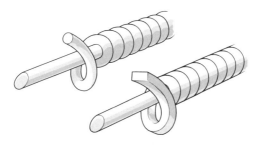

Round-wound and flat-wound strings.

Half-rounds

If you can't decide between flat- and round-wound strings, you may try *half-rounds* or *ground-wounds*, which offer a bit of both worlds. *Compound-wound* strings have multiple layers of winding.

BASS STRINGS

Bass strings are always wound. The extra mass of the winding allows them to sound as low as they do.

Flat or round

Bass strings come with the same wrap wire variations as guitar strings (see above). Round-wounds are by far the most popular choice. Flat-wounds are mainly used by jazz, reggae, and country bass players – but by some metal bassists too. For fretless basses, there are strings with a synthetic winding that reduces fingerboard wear.

Gauges

Most bassists use $^{040}/_{100}$ or $^{045}/_{105}$ string gauges, the lighter ones generally being preferred for slapping techniques, a brighter tone, and a faster attack. The heavier strings provide more depth, low end, and punch. The low B of a five- or six-string bass set usually ranges from .120 to .135.

Examples of bass string gauges.

Set name	1st string (G)	4th string (E)
Extra Light	030 (0.75 mm)	085 (2.1 mm)
Light	035	090
Medium	040	095, 100 or 105
Medium Heavy	045	105
Heavy	050 (1.25 mm)	110 (2.8 mm)

Different scales, different strings

Bass strings come in short, medium, long, and extra-long scale versions. If you put 'standard' long-scale strings on a shorter-scale instrument, their tension will be too low, resulting in a weak tone. Besides, fitting them in the tuning posts can be a problem.

HOW, HOW LONG, HOW MUCH?

Choosing strings, no matter how much you know about them, is mainly a matter of trying out lots of different types. In this process, it can help to jot down your comments on every new set of strings you try out (see page 141).

How

A certain type of string may sound great on one guitar, and less so on another. It may also sound great when you play it, and not if someone else does. The right choice depends on the instrument, your style of playing, your preferences…

Listen

How do you judge strings? By listening to their tone, but also by paying attention to their output and dynamic range, to how fast they respond, and to how responsive they are to the nuances of your playing. Also, listen if the set is balanced from string to string, in terms of volume and tone (see page 69).

From set to set
One of the reasons players tend to spend a little more on strings is that good strings are consistent from set to set: Each set of strings provides the same results.

Low B
For five- and six-string bassists, low B usually is the most critical string. Even at this low pitch – when played open – this string should produce a tight, focused, well-defined sound.

How long?
When strings get older, they start to sound dull and their intonation decreases, *i.e.*, they can't sound in tune over their entire range anymore. Also, they become harder to tune, and more likely to break. For an optimal performance, there are players who put on a new set of strings before each gig. Others, with less critical ears, less critical equipment, or less money, play the same strings for half a year or longer – and every time they do replace them, they're surprised by how bright their instrument can sound…

A month
If you play some eight to ten hours a week, try replacing your strings after a month. Do the new ones sound noticeably brighter? Then you may try replacing them even sooner next time. If you don't hear a difference, keep the next set on for two months, and see what happens. Another guideline: When they discolor, wound strings are past their best. They may not break for years, but a new set will improve your sound.

Bassists
Bass players use their strings longer than most guitarists – but if you slap a lot and want a bright, funky, percussive sound for that purpose you may want to replace yours much more often.

The more, the longer

The more you play, the more acidic your sweat, and the thinner your strings, the shorter they will last. You can make strings last longer by taking good care of them, as you will read in the next chapter.

Spare sets

The more often you change your strings, the less likely they are to give up on you unexpectedly. On the other hand, even a brand new string can break at the first chord. So always take one or two spare sets with you. High E-strings break most often, and some strings sets come with two of them.

Broken strings

If a plain string breaks, you can often replace just that one string. Replacing a single wound string will disturb the tonal balance of the strings: The new one sounds much brighter than the ones you've been playing for a while.

How much?

Most guitar strings cost between four and eight dollars a set. Bass string prices typically range from about twenty to forty dollars. Some companies provide much cheaper strings; others are much more expensive, featuring life-extending coatings, for example. Will the cheap ones work for you, or are the expensive ones more cost-effective? Try them out... Some companies use corrosion-inhibiting envelopes to package each string individually; others save the environment (and money) by using a single box or envelope for a set.

Brands

Examples of well-known string brands are Black Diamond, D'Addario, D'Aquisto, Darco, Dean Markley, DR, Elixir, Ernie Ball, GHS, LaBella, Rotosound, SIT, Thomastik-Infeld, and VMS. A few makes concentrate on bass or jazz strings, for example, but most of them make all kinds of strings. Quite a few makers also produce strings for other companies and brands. For example, many guitar and bass companies have their own strings, but they usually buy these strings elsewhere.

7. CLEANING AND CHANGING STRINGS

To get the best out of your instrument, you'll need to pay some extra attention to your strings – and that doesn't take much time or effort. Keeping them clean and fitting them properly is basically all there is to it. Tuning tips follow in Chapter 8.

The cleaner you keep your strings, the longer they will sound good. Clean strings also will help keep your fingerboard clean.

Perspiration
First of all, it really helps if you play with clean, dry hands only. Using a pH-neutral soap may reduce perspiration. If you sweat heavily, try rubbing your hands with talcum powder before you play. Don't use too much to prevent the powder from gumming up the wound strings and killing their tone.

Afterwards
No matter how clean your hands are, your fingers will leave natural oils and perspiration, so wipe the strings with a clean, dry, lint-free cloth (an old T-shirt, for example) when you're done playing.

Fingerboard
Don't forget to clean the underside of the strings too. Pull the cloth between the strings and the fingerboard, and run it up and down a couple of times. This also keeps the fingerboard and the frets from getting dirty, which saves time in maintenance.

String cleaners

You can make your strings last longer by using one of the many string cleaners available. These cleaners often leave a thin dirt-, oil-, and sweat-repellent film on the strings. Silicone-based cleaners also make your strings feel smoother. Other string products are specifically designed for that purpose. Before using any of these products, always read the instructions carefully. Most string cleaners shouldn't get on your instrument, so slide a piece of cardboard under your strings when applying them.

Coated strings

There are types of strings with a special coating that protects them from the influence of sweat, dust, and moisture. Their higher price pays for a longer life span, depending on, among other things, your chemical makeup.

A different brand or winding

If string cleaners and special coatings don't help to reduce the effect your perspiration has on your strings, try using strings with another type of winding (see page 72), or try using different brands or series.

Wound strings

Some players clean their wound strings by carefully pulling them up a little and then letting them snap back against the fingerboard a couple of times. This can help to get rid of gunk in the grooves of the windings.

Boiling strings

Many bass players clean their (expensive!) strings by boiling them for a few minutes, with or without a bit of vinegar, soda, detergent, or dishwashing liquid added to the water. Always rinse the strings well with plenty of cold water before getting them out of the pan: They do get extremely hot. Then dry them carefully in order to prevent oxidation. Boiled strings may break easier – not because they have been boiled, but because there may be kinks at the ends where they had previously been attached at the tuning posts.

Your instrument

To get your strings to last as long as possible, you need to take care of your instrument too. Rough spots on frets, or sharp edges at the nut or saddles, can cause excessive string wear. Some micro-fine sandpaper (2000 grit) may be all you need to smooth things out. A tip: Don't use steel wool, as bits of the 'wool' can migrate to the instrument's pickups where they can cause a variety of problems. Another tip: Leave precision jobs to your technician.

Check your strings
Oxidized and dirty strings can easily go out of tune, as do strings that have flat spots where they cross the frets – so they should be replaced. Check your strings from time to time, and run a finger underneath them too. If you want to release the string tension for that purpose, you may need to stabilize them again afterwards (see page 85).

REPLACING STRINGS
There are lots of ways to fit new strings. Whichever one you choose, as long as you do it right, tuning stability will improve.

One by one
When putting on a new set, it's usually best to change the strings one by one. This allows you to tune each new string to the one next to it, assuming that the instrument was – at least roughly – in tune to start with. On guitars with a floating bridge, replacing the strings one by one also keeps the bridge in its proper position. If the bridge's position changes, even ever so slightly, your intonation will be off (see page 109).

All at once, or two by two
If the fingerboard needs a thorough cleaning, it may be easier to take all the strings off. Alternatively, you can replace the strings two by two. This creates sufficient room for basic cleaning purposes.

On the table
Replacing strings is easiest when your guitar is flat on a table. A piece of foam plastic or a towel underneath prevents scratches and keeps the instrument from sliding away. Washing your hands before you start helps extend string life.

Removing strings

- Unwind the first string you want to replace (usually high E or low E), and take it off the tuning post. A *string winder* speeds up the process.

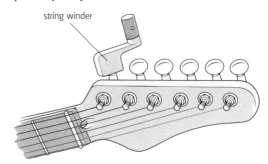

string winder

- To prevent the string from causing any damage when removing it at the other end, you can cut it close to the bridge. Strings should be completely slack before you cut them!
- If you have to remove the strings through slots in a plate on the back of the instrument, it's usually easiest to remove the plate. Leave it off to install the new strings, and then put it back on.

At the bridge

Feed each new string through the bridge or the stopbar tailpiece, and make sure its ball-end is in its proper position. Some types of bridges (*e.g.*, Floyd Rose) require that the ball-ends are cut off: The strings are locked with clamps.

At the tuning machines   Tipcode EGTR-009

On most electric guitars, the tuning posts have a hole on the side (top row, next page). To begin with, turn the appropriate post so that its hole is facing the string.

1. Feed the string into the hole.
2. Move it over and around the post once.
3. Start winding the string. Make sure there are no overlapping windings. On regular posts, make sure the string now runs underneath the hole.
4. When winding, keep the string under a little tension so it won't move at the bridge. Use your index finger to guide it through the slot in the nut.

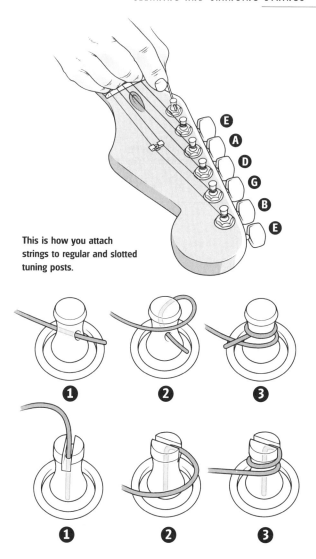

This is how you attach strings to regular and slotted tuning posts.

Slotted machines

Most bass guitars and some guitars have slotted tuning machines. They usually require you to cut the string to length before fitting it. (Only few models allow feeding the string right through them.) For guitars, cut each string an inch and a half beyond its post. Bass strings need a little more slack. Stick the end in the hole, move it around the post once, and start winding the string. Some players feed the string through the slot once more after the first winding.

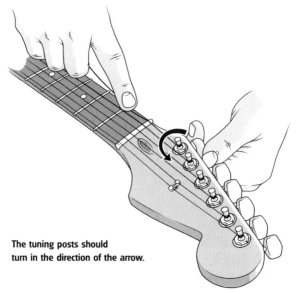

The tuning posts should
turn in the direction of the arrow.

Less wraps, more stability

Contrary to what many players believe, the number of wraps around the tuning post should be kept to a minimum: More wraps will decrease tuning stability. How come? When you bend your strings or ride the trem bar, the tension on the wraps changes. When you let go of the string or the trem bar, the wraps may not get back to their original position. The more wraps, the larger chances are that they don't – and as a result, the string(s) will be out of tune. As a rule of thumb, try to stick to a maximum of two wraps.

Locking machines

If you have locking tuning machines, the strings don't need to be wrapped around the posts at all, thus improving tuning stability. Bringing the strings to pitch usually requires less than one revolution of the tuning post.

Too long

Most strings are way too long when you buy them. You can cut them once they're in place, or before installing them, at about two inches past the tuning post. On traditional slotted tuning machines, you *have* to cut the strings to length beforehand. In other words: You will need a wire-cutter to replace strings, so always have one in your instrument case.

Locking nut

On guitars with a double-locking tremolo (see page 50), you need to tighten the locking nut once you've brought the strings to pitch. Once the nut has been locked, you can tune the strings with the fine-tuning machines at the bridge only. If you open the locking nut to use the regular tuning machines, you risk breaking the strings where they run under the lock.

Stabilizing strings   Tipcode EGTR-010

New strings tend to detune quickly: They need to stabilize. To speed up this process, gently 'stretch' each string a bit by sliding a finger under it and pulling up a little. Then bring it back to pitch. Repeat this for each string until its pitch doesn't change anymore.

Near the bridge

New strings can also detune because they are not yet seated correctly at the bridge saddles. You help them do so by gently pressing them down right next to the saddles.

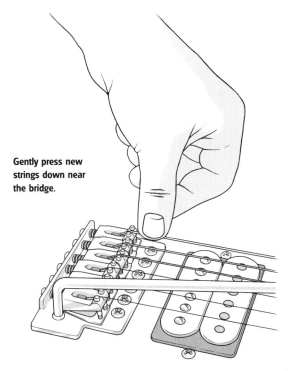

Gently press new strings down near the bridge.

String tips

· If your instrument has **string trees**, you should use them.

· **Prevent getting kinks in your strings** when installing them; kinks can cause bad intonation and even breakage.

· **Avoid mixing up strings**: Don't unpack a string until you're ready to put it on. Companies that don't package their strings individually attach labels to them.

· **Tuning too high** can damage your strings or your instrument. Refer to Chapter 8 for more information.

· To **improve tuning stability**, some players apply a tiny drop of Teflon lubricant in the slots of the nut. Some even include the saddles, and the strings' entries in the trem block.

· If you decide to remove all the strings from a **hollow-body guitar**, make sure that you know how (and where!) to replace the bridge. Also, put a cloth under the tailpiece to prevent it from damaging the finish when it comes loose.

8. ACCESSORIES

The main accessories for guitarists and bassists are cables, instrument cases or gig bags, straps, instrument stands, and picks. Here are their key details, and lots of helpful tips.

As long as you're still practicing at home, there's no reason to spend a lot of money on an instrument cable. When you start gigging, however, things change.

Long cables

The better your equipment – and your ears – the more important the quality of the cable will be, especially if you use one over fifteen feet long. The longer a cable gets, the more your clarity, definition, and dynamic range may suffer, unless you have an instrument with active electronics (see page 61). Spiral cables should usually be avoided.

Even your sound

Expensive cables are generally more robust and therefore more reliable, with thoroughly attached plugs and well-protected cable ends. Good internal shielding reduces the chance of microphonic noise, hum, and interference. Better cables can make for a better sound too. Provided the rest of your equipment is good enough, they can help enhance clarity, definition, high frequency response, and even gain.

Question

Some experts seriously question whether cables have any significant effect on the sound, though, while others even claim to hear the differences between the plugs of brand A or brand B…

Corrosion
Many cables use oxygen-free copper wire, which helps prevent corrosion. Gold-plated plugs do the same, but they're quite useless on instrument cables: The plating will wear off in no time.

Jacket
The ruggedness of the cable is in part determined by the material of the jacket. A good cable should also lay flat, with little or no 'memory,' and it shouldn't tangle or curl. Most cables have a synthetic jacket; others come with braided (woven) exteriors. Both types are available in a wide range of colors and designs, usually with a choice of straight and right-angle plugs.

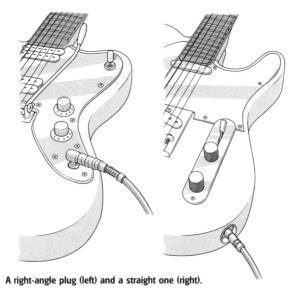

A right-angle plug (left) and a straight one (right).

Buzz
Some cables have special plugs that eliminate the buzz you hear when unplugging the cable from your instrument. These cables allow you to switch instruments silently without going to the amp to unplug your cord or turn the volume down. There are companies that make retrofittable cable accessories to the same effect.

Wireless

If you want to really move around onstage, you can consider a wireless system. A transmitter with an antenna is plugged into your instrument's output jack, and the receiver plugs into your amp or effects unit. Most wireless systems cost between two and six hundred dollars.

CASES AND BAGS

Your instrument will last longer if you pack it in a case or a gig bag. Apart from offering protection against damage on the road, a case or bag is also useful in keeping airborne dust and dirt from your instrument when you don't play.

Gig bags

Gig bags are available for as little as twenty-five dollars. More money buys you a thicker, stronger, shock-absorbent padding, and a tougher exterior; better zippers that are water-resistant and offer added protection against scratching your instrument; and wider, more comfortable adjustable shoulder or backpack straps. Most gig bags have extra pockets for spare strings, picks, an electronic tuner, cables, sheet music, or even an instrument stand or a music stand. Gig bags are less expensive, lighter, and easier to carry than most *hard-shell cases*, but a good hard-shell case offers better protection.

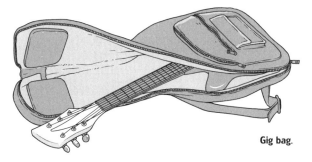

Gig bag.

Hard-shell cases

Cases come in different qualities too, starting at as little as fifty dollars for a case with a chipboard shell. Cases with plywood or molded plastic shells are stronger, but more expensive. A hard-shell case needs to perfectly fit your instrument. For example, some designs fit both instruments with and without tilted headstocks (see page 38); others don't.

Form-fitting or rectangular

Form-fitting cases usually offer less room for accessories than rectangular models, but most have at least one padded accessory compartment. The instrument is protected against scratches by a soft (usually plush or plush cotton) lining. Some cases have special features such as a support channel for the neck, or a built-in hygrometer and humidifier, which can be important for hollow-body instruments. Well-designed models have one or more thoroughly attached handles at strategic places.

Remove your strap

A tip: Always remove the strap from your instrument before putting it in its case or bag. One of the reasons to do so is that some types of strap material may damage your finish.

GUITAR STANDS

Intermission? Put your instrument in a good stand, rather than leaning it against a wall, your amp, or a piece of furniture.

Small or big

Some stands have been designed to fit a large accessory pocket, when folded up. Others don't fold up that compactly, but are designed for maximum stability. If you use more than one instrument, you can get yourself a multi-guitar stand; some cases even double as one!

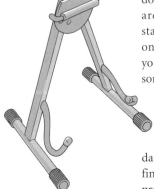

Collapsible guitar stand.

Cover the cushions

The padded arms and back rest of a guitar stand can damage some natural types of finish (*e.g.*, nitro-cellulose). To prevent this, simply cover these cushions with cotton cloth.

Neck support

Not all stands offer a separate neck support. The ones that do may have a security strap for extra safety.

The very smallest

The very smallest guitar 'stands' are plastic devices that are designed to lean the neck of the instrument in, keeping it from falling over. Some can simply be stuck to the seat of a chair, or to an amp or a table, for instance. Others are designed so that they can be plugged into a spare input or the headphone jack of your amp.

STRAPS

Guitar straps are available in numerous designs and materials, from basic five-dollar synthetic straps to padded, genuine leather models that cost ten times as much.

Quick release

Commonly, the instrument's strap buttons need to be pushed through the slits in the strap ends. To save time and to prevent the slits from wearing out, some straps have a quick-release system that leaves the strap ends attached to the instrument.

Security lock system with special strap buttons and retainers (Schaller).

Locking the strap

More advanced designs feature a positive, spring-loaded locking system. They require that the regular strap buttons are replaced by special strap buttons, and the strap gets a matching strap retainer at either end. These systems can be used on any guitar, with any standard strap. Installing them is a cinch.

Flush buttons

If you don't like the sight of strap buttons, you can have countersunk flush 'buttons' installed. Only a few companies provide these inset receivers and matching retainers as a standard item.

PICKS

Picks or *plectrums* come in numerous thicknesses, colors, shapes, sizes, and materials.

Picks in various sizes and materials, and with different surfaces.

Light or heavy

Pick thicknesses typically range from about .020" to .125" (0.5–3.2 mm); some are even thicker. Rhythm players tend to go for larger, softer, lighter-gauge picks which help produce bright, open sound. Lead players typically choose a thicker, harder type of pick, which enables them to play faster and more accurately, and produces a heavier, fuller, stronger, and better defined tone.

Picks, fingers, and fingerpicks

Bassists who use a pick generally use special, large bass picks – but most of them play with their fingers only. Some guitarists do so too, producing a very characteristic, warm, round type of sound. Other guitar players use finger picks, which are worn on individual fingers.

Materials

Most picks are synthetic. Celluloid is very popular, promoting a warm, musical tone. It's not very durable, however, unlike Acetal Polymer, a strong and resilient material generally known as Delrin. To make it less slippery, Delrin picks often have a matte finish. Other synthetics are used too, and so are wood, metal, horn, stone, and felt – for a wide range of sounds and effects. Natural materials are mainly used by hollow-body guitarists.

Anti-slip

Players with slippery fingers can choose from a wide variety of slip-proof picks, ranging from models with cork patches, concave knurled gripping areas, or an anti-slip hole.

Shape

How a pick plays and how it makes you sound also depends on the shape of the point. It can't hurt to experiment with pointed and rounded models. Playing will eventually change the shape of the point: Replace the pick, or use a file to reshape the point.

Special picks

Besides the regular models, there are three-way picks (three picks of different gauges in one); picks with notched edges that create a *grwwwww* sound when slid across wound strings; picks with a flexible 'hinge' in the middle; and many more variations.

Next to nothing

Most picks cost next to nothing. Experiment with different gauges and shapes until you find the one you like best. Cheap as they are, many picks have rough edges or other flaws. All it takes to finish them is a fine file or some fine sandpaper.

9. TUNING

Before you can start playing, you'll need to tune your instrument, or at least check whether it's still in tune. Tuning isn't that hard – though there's more to it than you may think... This chapter tells you the ins and outs of tuning with and without electronic tuners.

Tipcode EGTR-011 (guitar), EGTR-012 (bass)

The notes that guitar and bass strings are usually tuned to, are shown below (guitar) and on the next page (bass). Memory joggers for these notes are on page 7.

Extra strings

These diagrams also show the notes to which the extra string of a seven-string guitar is usually tuned (B1) and the extra strings of five-string (B0) and six-string basses (B0 and C3).

With and without tuners

Most guitarists and bassists tune their instrument with an *electronic tuner*, so that's where this chapter starts. As it's

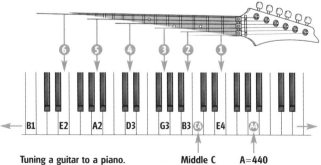

Tuning a guitar to a piano.　　　Middle C　　A=440

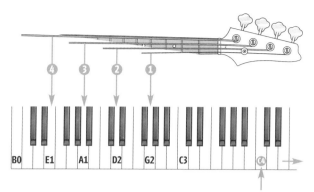

Tuning a bass guitar to a piano.   **Middle C**

good to be able to check the tuning with your ears too, and to be able to tune your instrument when your tuner breaks down, other tuning techniques are covered as well. Most players use a combination of these techniques.

Electronic tuners

To use an electronic tuner, you simply plug your cable in its input. The tuner's display will show you exactly whether a string is in tune, too high (*sharp*), or too low (*flat*).

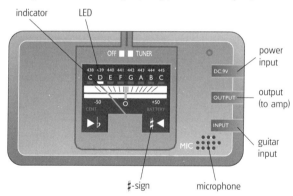

An automatic, chromatic electronic tuner (Seiko).

Basic

On the most basic type of tuner, you have to select the instrument you're going to tune (bass or guitar), and then the first string you will tune.

1. Select the instrument (check the tuner's manual).
2. Select low E.
3. Play low E, and don't play it too hard.

4. If the pointer shows that the string's pitch is too low, tighten the string a little. If it's too high, loosen it a bit.

5. When the pointer hits the middle of the scale, the string is in pitch.

6. Select and tune the other strings.

7. When all strings have been tuned, check them once more, starting at low E.

Chromatic tuners

Chromatic tuners automatically display which note they 'hear.' This type of tuner requires some basic knowledge of music theory. If, for example, the tuner displays an F when you play the low E string, you need to know that this means that the string sounds too high.

Faster

Assuming you do know all this, chromatic tuners work faster. Also, they allow you to use non-standard tunings (see page 103).

Numbered notes

Chromatic tuners often display numbered note names, as shown on the keyboard illustration above (*e.g.,* E2 is the guitar's low E). Manual tuners often display the strings' numbers (*e.g.,* 6E is the guitar's low E – the sixth string).

Your ears too

If you only use your eyes to tune your instrument, you won't train your ears to hear when a string goes out of tune. So it's good to listen to what you're doing. You can either connect the tuner's output to your amp, or plug your instrument directly into your amp and have the tuner's built-in microphone register the pitches you play.

Tuners

Electronic tuners are available from about twenty-five to a hundred dollars and more. For daily tuning purposes, a cheap one will do. If you also want to use it to adjust the intonation of your instrument, for example, you will want to get a better one that registers even the smallest pitch differences. Here are some other things to consider.

• Better tuners **respond faster** and may hold the reading a little longer.

- Better tuners offer a **wider tuning range**, up to seven octaves. Cheap tuners may not be able to accurately tune a five-string bass or a seven-string guitar, or register the high harmonics that are essential for adjusting the intonation of your instrument.
- Many good tuners also generate **reference pitches** (three or more octaves). The ones that do often have a separate headphone output.
- Also check how well the tuner can be read on a dark stage (some have an **illuminated display**), and whether it shuts off automatically after a while, to save batteries.
- Tuners with a mechanical pointer are usually slower and use more energy than the ones with an **LCD pointer**. LED pointers (small 'lights') are easy to read on dark stages.
- Some tuners double as a **metronome** (see page 20).
- Some **amplifiers and most multi-effects** feature a built-in tuner!

Output

Most tuners have an output, allowing you to leave the tuner between your instrument and your amp or effects. However, most players prefer not to.

A=440   Tipcode EGTR-013

If your guitar is in tune and you play the high E-string at the 5th fret, the string vibrates 440 times per second. This sounds the note A that most bands and orchestras tune to. It's known as A=440.

Higher or lower

Some bands may want to tune slightly higher or lower, or you may have to adjust your tuning to a piano that has been tuned a bit too high or too low. For this purpose, good tuners can be calibrated to alternate pitches (*e.g.*, from A=415 to A=450).

Fifty cents

Most tuners show the figures −50 and +50 on their displays. If the pointer indicates −25, the note you're playing is a quarter-step too low: *50 cents* equals a half-step (say, from E to F). More expensive tuners indicate pitch deviations digitally in steps of 1 cent. This is very helpful for precise tuning and intonation.

STRING TO STRING

A traditional way to tune your instrument is to compare the pitches of fretted and open strings.

Low E and A   Tipcode EGTR-014

Provided low E is in tune, play this string at the 5th fret. Then compare the open A-string to it. Adjust the A-string until it sounds the same pitch.

The other strings

When low A is in tune, play it at the 5th fret and adjust the open D-string to this pitch. Then tune the other strings according to the illustration below.

Guitarists only

For guitarists only: Note that you stop the strings at the 5th fret each time, except when you tune open B. This string is tuned to the G-string played at the 4th fret.

IV, V

In diagrams that represent a guitar neck and strings, it's common to indicate the frets with Roman numerals – IV is the 4th fret, V is the 5th, and so on.

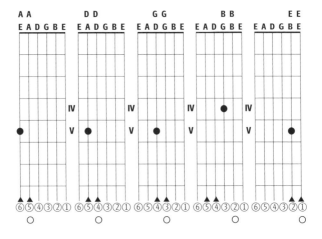

Tuning with fretted and open strings. Compare the two strings marked with the triangles below. The black dots indicate where to fret the strings. The open dots indicate the open strings. The resulting pitches are shown above the string names (EE, BB, etc.).

Bending strings

If you find it hard to hear whether a string sounds too high or too low, try bending the fretted string. This raises its pitch. If this makes it come closer to the open string's pitch, you need to tune the open string down – and vice versa.

Singing

You can also try to sing the notes you are comparing. You'll soon learn to 'feel' whether you need to sing higher or lower. Adjust the strings accordingly.

Tuning fork   Tipcode EGTR-015

If you don't have access to a tuner, a tuning fork will give you the reference you need to tune reliably, by ear. You simply hit this low-cost, two-pronged fork on your knee, for example, and then put the base of its stem on your instrument, or on a table top; this will enhance its volume.

In A or E

Most tuning forks produce the note A=440, because most musicians and bands tune to that note. For guitarists and bassists it's easier to get one that sounds an E, at the same pitch of the guitar's high E. Tune this string to the fork, and then use the illustration on the previous page in reverse order: First tune the B-string at the 5th fret to high E, then tune G to B, and so on. Alternatively, you can tune low E to high E, and proceed from there.

Tuning fork in A

If you have a *tuning fork* in A, adjust the high E-string at the 5th fret to that pitch.

Bass

To tune a bass to a tuning fork in A, play the G-string at the 14th fret. Your bass will sound an A an octave below the pitch of the tuning fork.

Too low or too high

If you play on your own, you don't need to tune to an exact reference pitch. If your instrument is tuned much too low, though, the low tension will make your strings rattle. If it's tuned way too high, your strings may break or you may damage your instrument.

HARMONICS

You can also compare string pitches using *harmonics* or *overtones*. This technique makes pitch differences a lot easier to hear.

Playing harmonics

It may take a little practice to play harmonics. Place a finger very lightly on the low E-string, barely touching it, exactly above the 12th fret. Then strike the string. The thin, high tone you'll hear is a harmonic. You'll hear harmonics best when using the bridge pickup only.

Fifth, seventh, and so on

Likewise, you can play harmonics at other frets. For tuning, you use the 5th, 7th, and 12th fret harmonics.

Five and seven   Tipcode EGTR-016

Tune the strings to each other by comparing the 5th fret harmonic of each lower-sounding string to the 7th fret harmonic of the adjacent higher-sounding string. Start with E and A, and then move up.

High B and E

Tuning the B-string is different, again. Compare the 7th fret harmonic of low E to open B, or to its 12th fret harmonic. Then tune high E: compare its 7th fret harmonic to the 5th fret harmonic on B. Finally, check your tuning. Also compare both E-strings, using harmonics on either both, or one of the strings.

B on the bass

To tune the low B-string on a bass, compare the 7th fret harmonic of low E to the 12th fret harmonic of the B-string.

Keep on ringing

Using harmonics makes tuning easier because the strings keep on ringing, so you can hear what's going on better. (If you fret them, the sound stops as soon as you let go of the string.)

Beats   Tipcode EGTR-017

Also, playing harmonics makes it easier to get two strings to sound at exactly the same pitch. Here's how: When the pitches you're comparing are very close, you will hear slower or faster 'waves.' These waves are known as *beats*. If you bring the two pitches even closer to each other, the beats will get slower. When they're gone, the two pitches are identical. If the beats get faster, you've gone too far, so back up and try again.

Tuning fork in A

If you have a tuning fork in A, adjust the A-string so that its 5th fret harmonic produces the exact same pitch.

INTERVALS AND CHORDS

Advanced players often tune their instrument by listening to the pitch differences (*intervals*) between the strings, without fretting them or playing harmonics. The A-string is supposed to sound a *perfect fourth* higher than the low E-string.

Amazing Grace

A perfect fourth is the interval that you hear when you sing the first two syllables of *Amazing Grace* or *Here Comes the Bride*. Sing the first syllable at the same pitch as your low E-string. Then tune the A-string to the pitch of the second syllable. The same interval is used when you go from strings A to D, D to G, and B to high E.

Oh When The Saints

The only interval that's different is the one from G to B. To tune the B-string to the G-string, sing the first two syllables of *Oh When the Saints Go Marching In*. This interval is called a *major third*.

Chords

Alternatively, you can check you guitar's tuning by playing chords and listening if they sound in tune. Preferably do this using one or more chords from the song you're about to play. However, you may find that while one chord sounds great, another one may sound completely off. How come? Read on…

One sounds great – but the others

If you tune your guitar so that the first-position E-major

chord sounds great, you'll find that that the first-position A-major chord sounds quite a bit less in tune (note the C♯ on the B-string!), and that D-major and C-major are even worse.

Solutions

The majority of players takes these and other natural pitch deviations for granted. The ones that don't can choose from a variety of solutions, ranging from having the nut replaced and the intonation adjusted according to a special system (*e.g.*, Buzz Feiten), to having two special frets with a small curve fitted (*e.g.*, Fretwave), or using special nuts (*e.g.*, Earvana). Some companies feature one of these solutions as a standard item.

MORE TUNING TIPS

- Always tune a string by **increasing its tension**. If it's too high, loosen it a bit and then tune up from there. It's easier to hear what you're doing that way, and it helps improve tuning stability.
- You can tune your guitar or bass to a **pitch pipe**. Pitch pipes cost next to nothing, but they do go out of tune rather easily.
- You can also tune all your strings to the corresponding notes of a **keyboard instrument**.
- Do your strings **go out of tune** quickly, or is it hard to get them in tune? That could be the result of too many windings around the tuning post (see page 84), worn strings, poor adjustment, too narrow nut slots, worn bridge saddles, a bad tremolo... Have your instrument checked by an expert, if you can't find the culprit(s!) yourself.
- Is tuning hard because the **strings stick in the slots** of the nut? This can be solved temporarily by frequently pressing the strings right behind the nut. Tune, press, listen, tune... Another solution is to run the point of a lead pencil in the slots. Ultimately, however, the nut should be replaced (see page 53) or adjusted.
- Does your guitar go out of tune after severe string bends or trem use? **Flexing the tremolo bar** once or twice may bring you back in tune.
- Do you have a tremolo bridge with **fine-tuning**

machines (*e.g.*, Floyd Rose)? Then avoid leaning on the bridge when tuning. Tune, let go of the fine-tuning machine, listen, tune again if necessary, and so on.

DIFFERENT TUNINGS

Some heavy metal and other guitarists tune a half-step or more lower than the regular tuning. Basses can be tuned differently too. You can also raise the pitch of your strings by using a capo. Another tuning alternative is to use an *open tuning*.

Half-step, whole-step

Tuning a guitar lower than normal makes for a heavier, fatter, thicker sound. Also, the lower tension makes string bending easier. Combined with heavier-gauge strings, the sound becomes even punchier. Some players tune a half-step lower (E♭, A♭, D♭, G♭, B♭, E♭); others a whole step (D, G, C, F, A, D; sometimes referred to as a *D-neck*). On 7-string jazz guitars, low B is often tuned down to an A.

Even lower

If you tune a regular guitar even lower, your strings will flop – except on guitars built for such low tunings (page 119).

Adjustments

Using any of these lower *drop tunings* may require extra adjustments, as described in Chapter 10.

D-tuners and B-benders

For some songs, it can be useful to extend the range of your bass or guitar to low D, which means tuning the low E-string a whole-step down. This drop-D tuning is easiest if your instrument has a *D-tuner*. A few instruments come with such a device; you can also have one retrofitted. A similar device, the *B-bender*, which raises the B, is much rarer.

B to C

The lowest string on five- and six-string basses (low B) often sounds a bit weak, flabby, or indistinct. Some players make it sound punchier and tighter by tuning it a half-step up, from B to C.

A capo

For some songs, it can be easy to raise the pitch of your guitar entirely. You do so with a *capo* – a clamp that you simply attach at the required fret. If, for example, you want to raise the pitch a whole-step, you use it at the second fret, as shown below.

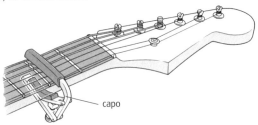

capo

Always attach a capo close to the fret, where you would normally put your fingers. This type of capo can be mounted from the other side of the neck too (Shubb).

Open tunings

Many players in a variety of styles use *open tunings*, meaning that the *open* strings are tuned to produce a certain chord. This allows you to play entire songs by simple putting a finger across all six strings (known as a *barre*), and sliding from chord to chord without using any difficult fingerings.

Two examples

Tuning your strings to D, G, D, G, B, and D (from thick to thin), for example, produces a G-major chord. Tuned to E, A, E, A, C♯, and E, the open strings ring an A-major chord.

10. MAINTENANCE

Apart from cleaning, guitars and basses do not require a lot of maintenance. There are some minor adjustments you can easily do yourself. Other types of adjustment are best left to an expert. This chapter ends with some additional tips for on the road.

If you wipe your guitar – body, strings, neck – with a clean, soft, lint-free cloth each time you're done playing, it won't require much additional cleaning. When it does need extra attention, there are plenty of special cleaners to choose from.

Bodies and lacquered fingerboards

Most guitar and bass bodies have a polyurethane or nitrocellulose lacquer finish, which can be cleaned and restored to its original shine with most available guitar cleaners. The same goes for polyurethane lacquered fingerboards (*i.e.*, most maple fingerboards).

Which cleaner?

Some cleaners are a cream-like substance, others are sprays. Some polish better, others clean better. Yet another product is most effective at reducing the cloudiness caused by wax buildup of old cleaners. Most cleaners can also be used to clean your instrument's hardware, knobs, and pickguard. Ask your dealer for advice, and try different cleaners to find which one works best for you. Always read the instructions first, and begin by trying a bit on a less visible section of your instrument. One more tip: Use a soft brush or cloth to remove any dust before applying a cleaner. Dust scratches, really!

Open pore

Special finishes may need special cleaners. Instruments with a wax or oil finish that leaves the pores of the wood open can usually be treated with the same substances that are used for non-lacquered fingerboards, such as lemon oil or fingerboard conditioner. Some experts advise beeswax. You can also try a mild guitar cleaner. If you're not sure what to use, ask your dealer for advice. Unfortunately, most companies do not include a cleaning manual with their instruments.

Don't

Experimenting with cleaners that weren't designed for musical instruments can damage your (bass) guitar – but you should know that many players and technicians use furniture or automotive polishes with great results, and at a low price. Ask around!

The knobs

If the body needs to be cleaned thoroughly, it's good to remove not only the strings, but the knobs too. Some knobs have a small screw that you should loosen first; others are clamped on a split shaft. If you can't pull them off with your fingers, you may try using a screwdriver to push them upward, bit by bit, using a piece of cardboard to protect the body – but it's usually safer to have your technician do it.

Non-lacquered fingerboards

When you can clearly see your finger marks on a non-lacquered fingerboard, you're late cleaning it. Use a special fingerboard conditioner or lemon oil. Apart from cleaning the fingerboard, they also replenish the oils in the wood and prevent it from drying out. Do take all the strings off before treating the fingerboard, as strings and oil don't match, and again, read the instructions before using any type of cleaner or oil.

Brands

Guitar cleaners and other maintenance products are supplied by companies like D'Andrea, Dunlop, Number One, GHS, and Kyser, and some guitar manufacturers have their own cleaners.

Cloths, brushes, and Q-tips

Apart from a few lint-free cloths (one to apply each type of cleaner or oil, another one to rub or buff), you can use a soft toothbrush, a paintbrush, or Q-Tips to get into the nooks and crannies of your instrument.

Scratchy controls

To clean scratchy controls, you need to expose the actual potentiometers to be able to treat them with a special type of spray cleaner. Such cleaners are available in most hardware and electronics stores. If you're not absolutely sure of how to handle this, let your dealer clean the pots and pickup selector for you.

ADJUSTMENTS

A well-adjusted guitar or bass is easier to play and easier to tune, and it sounds better too. This section covers the main adjustment jobs, including action or string height, the neck, tremolo, intonation, pickup height, and the stopbar. Some of these adjustments require more experience and skill than you may think, so don't do anything yourself unless you're absolutely sure you can handle it.

ACTION

The *action* or *string height* is the distance between the strings and the frets. It may need to be adjusted because you'd like to experiment with a higher or a lower action, because of a switch to heavier- or lighter-gauge strings (heavier strings raise the action; lighter-gauge strings lower the action), or because of seasonal changes (dry winter air makes wood contract, which can influence the action).

Saddles, nut, and neck

The action can be adjusted by lowering or raising the saddle(s) or the nut, by adjusting the neck with the built-in truss rod, or by any combination of these three. Deciding what needs to be done requires an expert eye. For example, raising the action by adjusting the bridge saddles may have no use if the nut or the neck adjustment do not suit the string height you have in mind.

Low or high

If you go for speed and easy playability, you'll probably prefer a relatively low action. A higher action makes playing a bit heavier, but it helps produce a better tone and more sustain, and cleaner, buzz-free chords, especially if you hit the strings hard. For bassists, slapping is easier with a relatively low action. If you go for extra volume and a large dynamic range, you may try setting the action a bit higher.

Too low

If the action is set too low, strings will rattle against the frets, or choke when you bend them. Also, the string above the one you are bending may creep under your fingers and kill the tone.

Starting point

As a starting point, high E should be at least 0.05" (³⁄₆₄" or 1.2 mm) above the 12th fret, and low E about 0.08" (2 mm). Bass guitar strings need more room to move, of course, up to some 0.110 (2.8 mm) for low E. You can use drill bits to check the action of your instrument. (Carefully stick them between the relevant fret and string.)

Saddles

Most guitars and basses have individually adjustable saddles (one per string); some have one saddle per two strings; others have a bridge that can be raised or lowered entirely. The latter design requires you to release the tension of the strings before adjusting it.

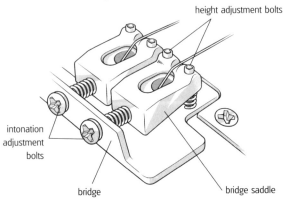

Section of a bridge with individually adjustable saddles.

The neck

The neck and fingerboard are very slightly concave along their length, dipping a little between headstock and body. This *neck relief* helps prevent the strings from buzzing.

Check

You can check the neck relief by fretting low E at both the 1st and the 15th frets. (Using a capo at the 1st fret makes this a lot easier.) When held down at these two points, there should be a small gap between the string and the middle frets. If there isn't, your neck is either flat or convex, and strings may rattle. If the gap is larger than about 0.040" (1 mm), the instrument will be quite hard to play. In both cases, the neck should be adjusted with its truss rod. This is best left to a technician.

S-necks and kinks

Some necks have a slight S-shape, being concave up to the 8th fret, and then convex; others have a kink in the 13th/15th fret area, which can result in choking strings when bending them at those and higher frets. Both problems require an expert.

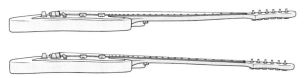

The neck of the first guitar is too concave, the other one is convex.

TREMOLO

Tremolo adjustment is adjusting the balance between the strings that pull on one side, and the springs that pull on the other. This is critically important for both the playability and the sound of your instrument. Switching to lighter or heavier strings usually requires adjusting the tremolo, and it even may need to be adjusted when switching from one string brand to another.

INTONATION

On most instruments, the bridge saddles can be adjusted lengthwise. This adjustment, the *intonation*, is important

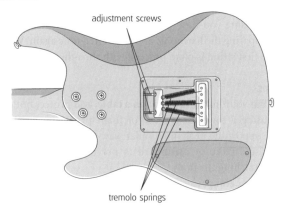

adjustment screws

tremolo springs

Tremolo springs should be well-adjusted too.

for how well in tune the instrument sounds over its entire range. Adjusting the intonation is not very difficult, technically speaking, but it does require a very sensitive tuner or a pair of well-trained ears.

Moving the saddles
You set the intonation by moving the saddles forward or backward. On some bridges this is easier than on others.

The 12th harmonic, the 12th fret   Tipcode EGTR-018
The most basic and best-known way to set the intonation is to adjust each string so the pitch of its 12th fret harmonic is identical to the pitch when you fret the string at that point.
1. Tune your instrument.
2. Play the 12th fret harmonic of the low E (see page 100).
3. Play the low E at the 12th fret.
4. Compare the two pitches.

Higher or lower
If the fretted note sounds higher than the harmonic, the distance between the fret and the saddle is too short. The solution is to move the saddle backward, away from the fret. If the fretted note sounds lower, you need to move the saddle forward, toward the pickups.

Move, tune, compare   Tipcode EGTR-019
Moving the saddle forward or backward, even ever so slightly, will make the pitch drop or rise considerably.

Make sure you tune the string to its proper pitch before comparing the harmonic and the fretted note again. When the first string is okay, proceed with the other strings.

Tips

- Put your instrument **flat on a table**, and protect both by using a towel or a piece of foam plastic underneath. Support the neck in a similar way.
- Use a piece of **cardboard** to prevent your tools from scratching the body.
- When comparing the pitches, try **not to vary the way** you pluck and fret the strings.
- To **prevent the strings from binding** at the nut or the saddles, stretch them every time you've moved the saddle.
- The intonation can be set properly only when your **strings are in prime condition**: clean, and preferably new.
- Make it a habit to check and adjust your intonation **after every string change**.
- Note that it's close to impossible to get a string to sound **exactly the same pitch** when comparing the fretted note and the harmonic at that fret – but you can get close.
- You can also check intonation by comparing **the open string** to the 12th harmonic of each string!

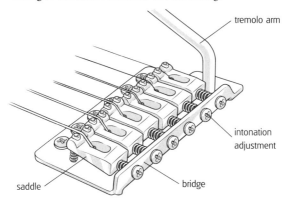

tremolo arm

intonation adjustment

saddle

bridge

The intonation is adjusted by moving the saddles lengthwise, changing the length of each string.

Another one

A more advanced way to adjust intonation is not to compare a harmonic and a fretted note per string, but to go from string to string. Here's how:

1. The 5th fret harmonic of low E should produce the same pitch as the A-string played at the 19th fret. Adjust the A-string saddle to match the harmonic. Proceed likewise with the other strings (except for the B-string, which should be played at the 20th fret).

2. Then compare the 7th fret harmonic of low E to the A-string's 14th fretted note. You will probably find that the fretted note is a bit flat – so you can raise it ever so slightly by moving the saddle forward, aiming for the 'perfect middle.' Adjust the other strings likewise (except for the B-string, which should be played at the 15th fret).

3. Finally, adjust the low-E saddle by comparing the 12th fret harmonic on the A-string to low E's 17th fretted note.

Not so easy

Not all bridge designs allow for an easy adjustment of the intonation. Ask your dealer for advice. Properly adjusting a one-piece, floating bridge is an expert's job.

PICKUP HEIGHT

Pickup height can be adjusted – sometimes even per string. If a pickup is set too low, you will have low output, and your dynamic range and brightness will suffer. If you move it closer to the strings, attack and output will increase, but the tone may become harsh and edgy. What's worse, the magnet(s) may keep the strings from vibrating properly. This is commonly known as *string pull*.

Extreme

In the extreme case (strong magnet, close to the strings), string pull can make strings clatter against the fingerboard. In a milder case, string pull may produce false overtones.

Warble

The mildest form of string pull adds a very slight 'warble' to the tone, a bit like what a *chorus* does. Some guitarists find this an indispensable element of their tone.

Yourself

Adjusting pickup height is quite easy. Most players will try to find the height that gives them maximum output without string pull. Some like to set the bridge pickup very high for solos, and the neck pickup pretty low for chord playing; or you can try setting different heights on the treble and bass sides.

Thumb rest

Bass players often use one of their pickups as a thumb rest. For that purpose, you should be able to fasten the pickups in both high and low positions.

OTHER ADJUSTMENTS

If your guitar has a stopbar tailpiece, you can raise it to reduce the pressure of the strings on the bridge saddles. This makes for a 'singing' timbre with additional overtones. Lowering the stopbar increases the string pressure. This promotes a tighter, brighter, punchier sound, with more attack. However, the reduced angle at the bridge also increases the risk of breaking strings.

INTERFERENCE

Almost all guitars and bass guitars buzz, hum, or hiss to some extent. If there's too much noise, the culprit may be your cable, your instrument, your amp, or fluorescent lighting, a mains outlet, a nearby railroad line, the stage lighting – you name it.

Cable, instrument, amp?

The easiest way to check the cable is by replacing it with your backup cable. Likewise, you can check your instrument by replacing it with another bass or guitar, using the same amp and cable.

The instrument

A noisy instrument can be the result of bad connections, a worn output jack, or lack of shielding. Both cable and instrument should be shielded, the latter by using grounded metal foil or conductive paint in the body cavities. Three tips: Humbucking pickups are less noisy than single-coil pickups; active pickups are even quieter; distortion pedals amplify everything, noise included.

Plugs and noice suppressors

If the interference is not in your equipment, you can try using another mains outlet, or putting the plug in the other way round (if the type of plug in your country allows for that). If you're near a power station, a railroad, or other high-voltage cables, then special noise suppression equipment may be required.

ON THE ROAD

- Make sure you bring along **spare strings, picks, and a cable**. Don't forget spare batteries for instruments with active electronics, and for effects and tuners.
- Never leave your equipment in a car **unattended**.
- In a car, the best place for your instrument is usually on the floor **between the back and front seats**.
- Wooden instruments don't like **sudden changes in temperature and humidity**. If it's cold outside, it's best to allow your instrument to adjust to room temperature by leaving it in its case for a while. Hollow-body instruments are more vulnerable than solidbodies, in every respect.
- Never leave your instrument where it can get **too hot**.
- Extremely **dry air** (*e.g.*, wintertime, air conditioning, central heating) can make wood crack. Humid air can make strings and electronics oxidize. The best humidity, both for instruments and people, is about 40 to 60%.
- Flying out? Then it's best to carry your instrument as **hand luggage**, if that's allowed.
- If your guitar has a **serial number**, you'll probably find it on the back of the head, or on the label, or somewhere else inside the body. Jot it down, preferably before your instrument is stolen or lost. There's room to do so on pages 140–141.
- Consider **insuring your instrument**, especially if you're taking it on the road – which includes visiting your teacher. Musical instruments fall under the 'valuables' insurance category. A regular homeowner insurance policy will not cover all possible damage, whether it occurs at home, on the road, in the studio, or onstage.

11. BACK IN TIME

The solid-body guitar and bass have only been around since the 1950s. Right from the start, they have played a leading role in a wide variety of musical styles – and they still do.

Even though they are different in many ways, the electric guitar clearly stems from its acoustic namesake. The history of the acoustic guitar starts thousands of years ago, when supper was still something you hunted. Humans soon discovered that shooting an arrow produces a tone, due to the vibration of the string. Many years later, someone found a way to amplify that sound by attaching a gourd to the bow. That was the first forefather of the guitar.

Luthier

Numerous variations on the first string instruments have appeared all around the world, eventually leading to the modern-day guitar. One of its best-known ancestors is the medieval lute, which explains why guitar makers are still referred to as *luthiers*. The first instruments resembling today's acoustic guitar emerged in the sixteenth century.

Seventeenth century guitar with five pairs of strings.

115

These guitars often had five single or double strings, lacking a low E.

The classical guitar
Around 1850, the Spanish luthier Antonio de Torres combined a slightly bigger soundbox with an improved bracing pattern (*fan-bracing*) and a new scale, creating the guitar on which all modern classical, nylon-string guitars are based.

The steel-string guitar
Around the same time, the American guitar maker George Friedrich Martin designed the forerunner of today's steel-string acoustic guitar. This instrument had a larger soundbox than the nylon-string guitar, and a special bracing system (*X-bracing*).

Frying pan
The instrument that is considered to be the first electric guitar was built in the early 1930s by George D. Beauchamp. This 'Frying Pan' was made for Adolph Rickenbacker.

Les Paul and Paul Bigsby
Some ten years later, guitarist Les Paul made one of the earliest solid-body guitars by modifying an Epiphone guitar. The guitar that Paul Bigsby helped create around 1947 was another step closer to the modern solidbody. In 1948, Gibson made the first guitars with two pickups, allowing for previously unknown tonal variations.

Fender Broadcaster
In 1950, Fender introduced the world's first mass-produced solid-body electric. This Leo Fender design, first called Broadcaster and then renamed Telecaster, is still available.

Strat
The best-known electric guitar design is Fender's Stratocaster, introduced in 1954. Many, many guitars have been based on this instrument, which is still available in many different versions and price ranges.

Again: Les Paul
Shortly later, Gibson introduced the humbucking pickup.

This soon became the standard pickup on the famous Gibson Les Paul guitars (1952) – another design that never left the scene.

Bass guitars

After Leo Fender built his first solid-body guitars, he realized he could make bass guitars the same way. This would free the double-bassist from the huge 'doghouse' and provide loads of extra volume too.

Precise

Double basses don't have frets, but Fender used frets on the electric bass guitars. The name of the first electric basses, Precision, refers to the 'precise' way of playing allowed by using frets.

Then and now

Most of today's electric guitars and basses are largely based on the original designs – and many players would love to have and play an instrument from that era. On the other hand, the guitar industry has come up with numerous inventions, improvements, and alterations: active electronics, noiseless pickups, graphite reinforcements, dual truss rods, new body and neck materials, headless body designs, locking tremolos, flush strap locks, locking tuning machines, coated strings, D-tuners, guitar synthesizers, and so on. And of course, the solid-body concept has always allowed for the wildest body designs. Just one example is Gibson's Flying V, which dates back to 1958 – and the body design is still on the market.

A Gibson Flying V from 1958.

12. THE FAMILY

Electric guitars and basses belong to the family of string instruments. Within that family they're usually referred to as fretted instruments, contrary to violins, for example. This chapter covers just a few of the many different guitars and basses, both electric and acoustic.

There are basses with rubber strings, electric travel guitars with an onboard amp and speakers, guitars with built-in programmable tuning systems, basses with violin-like bodies, guitars with touch-sensitive sensors rather than strings, and instruments with five necks – but they're rare. Much more common variations include double-neck instruments, multi-string models, headless designs, and guitars and basses with nonstandard scales.

Violin bass (Höfner).

Double-necks

Double-neck instruments come in various configurations – a six-string and a twelve-string guitar neck, for example; or a six-string fretted and a four-string fretless bass neck; or a six-string electric and a six-string acoustic instrument.

More strings

Though they're less common than acoustic twelve-string guitars, electric twelve-string instruments are available. So are ten-string models, on which the four top strings are doubled to produce a richer, fuller sound.

A Gibson Double-Neck: One neck has six strings, the other twelve.

Multi-string basses

Since the 1980s, five-string basses have become increasingly popular, and there are plenty of six-string models around too. Some companies also built basses with even more strings – seven, eight, or nine. Other designs feature both bass and guitar strings. One example is an eight-string instrument with a guitar string next to each bass string. This makes each note sound as if it's played simultaneously on a bass and a guitar. Twelve-string basses, with two extra guitar strings for each bass string, are also available. Other bassists prefer to play real bass notes only. For them, three-string basses have been built, leaving out the G-string.

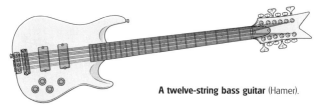

A twelve-string bass guitar (Hamer).

Lower tunings

To allow for really low guitar tunings without flopping strings, a few companies make instruments with extra long scales. Some call them *baritone guitars*; other names refer to the 'subsonic' character of the instruments, or to the lowered 'drop' tuning. Scale lengths vary from a little under 27" to over 30". One popular way to tune such a guitar is as if it were a seven-string instrument, leaving out high E (B, E, A, D, G, B). Players who want to be able to use the familiar fingerings tune them to B, E, A, D, F♯, B.

Higher tunings

Conversely, some bass guitars have been designed for higher tunings. Two examples are the piccolo bass, usually tuned to the same notes as the four lowest-sounding guitar strings, and the tenor bass, tuned to A, D, G, C (a fourth above a regular bass).

Headless

In the early 1980s, Ned Steinberger developed a bass guitar which had the tuning machines at the tail, making the headstock redundant. This design paved the way for more headless instruments, both basses and guitars. Instead of wood, Steinberger used a reinforced glass and carbon fiber resin.

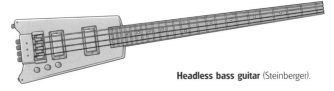

Headless bass guitar (Steinberger).

Upright electrics   Tipcode EGTR-020

The electric bass guitar is of course directly related to the double bass – which, at the same time, is a completely different instrument. Some companies produce a cross between both extremes, with the upright playing position, the long-scale neck, and the fretless fingerboard of a double bass, and the pickup and the solid or chambered body of an electric bass guitar.

ACOUSTIC GUITARS

Acoustic guitars are designed to be played acoustically – without an amplifier, that is. The soundbox amplifies the sound of the strings.

Classical, nylon strings   Tipcode EGTR-021

The classical, nylon-string, or 'Spanish' guitar is used mainly but not exclusively for classical music. The nylon strings (three wound, three plain) make for a warm, colorful sound. There is little or no variation in body size, scale, or other dimensions, apart from some special designs and down-sized models for children.

Steel-string guitars

The steel-string guitar, an American invention, typically has a larger soundbox than the classical guitar – but there are models with small bodies too. To distinguish them from acoustic guitars with an arched top, these acoustic steel-string instruments are also known as *flat-top guitars*.

Two acoustic guitars: a nylon-string Spanish guitar (top), and a steel-string guitar.

ACOUSTIC/ELECTRIC (BASS) GUITARS

To allow acoustic guitars and bass guitars to be used on larger stages and in electric bands, many of them have a pickup, usually hidden in the bridge. These instruments are commonly known as acoustic/electrics (or electro-acoustics, etc.).

Piezo pickups

Most acoustic/electric guitars and basses use a *piezo* or *piezo-electric pickup*. This type of pickup is pressure-sensitive: It picks up the pressure variations caused by the vibrations of the strings, and converts those to electric signals. Contrary to magnetic pickups, piezo pickups work with nylon strings as well. Their relatively weak signal is boosted by a small preamp that is built into the soundbox. Piezo pickups are used on some electric guitars and basses too (see page 62).

121

Controls

Volume and tone controls are usually located in a control panel on the instrument's left upper bout. Some of these systems also feature built-in effects, or a tuner.

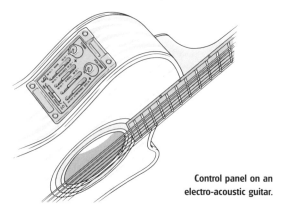

Control panel on an electro-acoustic guitar.

Acoustic or electric?

Many guitars are neither fully electric nor completely acoustic. An example would be the type of 'classic electric' guitar with a shallow, almost solid body (sometimes referred to as a *semi-solid*) and a piezo pickup; or an instrument that plays like an electric guitar yet has a very acoustic sound; or an acoustic/electric with a rather shallow body in the shape of a well-known solidbody… The names of such guitars often indicate what they're about: Classic Electric (Gibson), Acousticaster (Godin), Stratacoustic (Fender), and Ampli-Coustic (Renaissance) are just some examples.

Tipbook Acoustic Guitar

More information about acoustic and acoustic/electric guitars can be found in *Tipbook Acoustic Guitar*.

MORE FRETTED INSTRUMENTS

Guitars and bass guitars are not the only fretted instruments. Two other examples are the *banjo* (four or five strings, round soundbox, a plastic 'drumhead' rather than a wooden top, steel strings) and the *mandolin* (small soundbox in a variety of shapes, flat or arched top, four pairs of steel strings).

A five-string banjo.

Steel guitar

The electric steel guitar is played horizontally, strings facing up, either on the player's lap or mounted on a frame. The strings are played with a pick; a slide is used instead of fretting the strings. Most steel guitars have pedals that can be used to change pitch or tunings. Due to its origins, the instrument is also known as *Hawaiian guitar*.

Chapman Stick

An interesting cross between a guitar, a bass, and a piano is the Chapman Stick, introduced in the mid-1970s. With eight to twelve strings that are tapped rather than plucked or strummed, the instrument allows you to simultaneously play a melody or a solo, a bass part and chords – just like a pianist. Other makers have more recently introduced similar instruments, some with even more strings.

Balalaika, saz...

Fretted instruments are used in many other cultures as well. The Russian *balalaika*, for example, with its large, triangular soundbox; or the Turkish *saz-baglama*, with adjustable(!) frets and a small, pear-shaped body; or the Greek four-course (eight strings in four pairs) *bouzouki*.

13. HOW THEY'RE MADE

In fully-automated plants as well as hands-on small workshops, the basic principles of making a traditional, wood-bodied guitar or bass are essentially the same.

Tipcode EGTR-022

'Solid' bodies usually look like they're made of a single piece of wood, but that's rarely the case. Typically, a body consists of two or more blocks of wood, or it's laminated. Instruments with a transparent finish usually have a separate top ply as well.

Bookmatched

In the higher price ranges, two-piece bodies and guitar tops are often bookmatched: A single piece of wood is split so that it can be folded open like a book. Then, the halves (their grains showing a matching, mirror image) are glued together. As well as looking good, bookmatching makes the instrument highly resistant to warping.

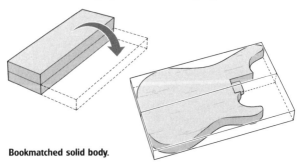

Bookmatched solid body.

Photo

On less expensive instruments with a see-through finish,

the top may look like (bookmatched) wood, but it's actually a photo, as described on page 30.

Handwork or machines
Shaping the body can involve anything from old-fashioned handwork to using advanced, computer-controlled machinery, such as CNC routing machines to cut the cavities for the pickups and potentiometers, as well as the pocket for the neck.

The neck
The neck, also, is often made of several pieces of wood, using similar wood-working machines. On through-neck instruments, the body consists of two 'wings' that are glued to the neck. Presses are used to properly seat the frets, which are laid into carefully positioned slots.

Finishing
Finishing the body and the neck often involves applying various coats, each one preceded by carefully sanding the wood. At the end, most instruments are buffed to a high-gloss finish.

Assembly
Assembling the instrument includes gluing or screwing the neck onto the body, and installing the pickups and other electronic components, the hardware, and the strings. Most companies buy both the electronics and the hardware from other sources.

DIY
As all components (necks, bodies, pickguards – you name it) are easily available, electric guitars are among the easiest instruments to make yourself. However, don't be disappointed if a homemade guitar costs more, and sounds and looks worse than one that you buy off the shelf.

Hollow-body instruments
Expensive hollow-body guitars have bookmatched tops and backs that are hand-carved in shape – a time-consuming affair. The sides of the soundbox (the ribs) are made with the help of a mold. Thin linings help to hold the top, sides, and back together.

14. BRANDS

There are hundreds of guitar companies and individual makers. This chapter introduces you to some of the main brands* you'll come across.

The guitar and bass market is quite confusing. Not only because there are so many brand names, but also because company A produces guitars for brands B and C, while brand B has another range of instruments made by company D…

One brand, several factories

Many guitar companies, both large and small, have their instruments made in various countries – their budget series in Asia, the intermediate instruments in the Czech Republic or Mexico, and the professional instruments in the US, for example.

One factory, several brands

Many – mainly Asian – manufacturers produce instruments and parts for several brands, one of them being their own 'house' brand. These companies also supply dealers who sell instruments under their private brand names.

An indication

Some of the brands listed in this chapter can be found in pretty much every music store; most are much rarer. By the time you read these pages, certain companies may have

---

* *Trademarks and/or user names have been used in this book solely to identify the products or instruments discussed. Such use does not identify endorsement by or affiliation with the trademark owner(s).*

disappeared; others may have been introduced; brand names may have been sold to other companies; and guitar makers may have added instruments in other prices ranges to their catalog(s). In other words, the following information is merely an indication, and it's by no means intended to be complete. Please refer to the specialized magazines and websites (see pages 137–139) for up-to-date information.

All price ranges

A few companies present instruments in pretty much all price ranges. These are the best-known names in the guitar industry. Most of them market acoustic guitars, amplifiers, effects, strings, and other musical products as well.

Fender and Squier

The American company Fender was the first manufacturer to produce solid-body guitars and basses. The products are made in various countries, including the US, China, and Mexico. The Squier brand name, owned by Fender, is mainly used for lower-priced instruments. Other Fender brand names include Guild and DeArmond (see below).

Gibson and Epiphone

Gibson, founded in 1902, is another classic name. In the early 1930s, Gibson built its first semi-acoustic instrument, the Electric Spanish Guitar. The Gibson name is found on professional guitars only. The company's low-budget and intermediate instruments are marketed under the Epiphone name.

Japan

Two of the main Japanese brand names are **Ibanez** and **Yamaha**. Ibanez was originally a Spanish guitar distributed by Hoshino, a company that started selling sheet music in 1908. Some fifty years later, Hoshino introduced the first original Japanese electric Ibanez guitars. Yamaha started as a one-man organ factory in 1889 and evolved into the world's largest manufacturer of musical instruments.

American companies

Most other companies that market instruments in various price ranges are American by origin. Among them are

BC Rich, Gretsch, Hamer, Jackson, Peavey, Schecter, Washburn, and Warrior. Their professional models are usually US-made; the less expensive instruments are often made overseas.

Starting low

Some examples of companies that focus on low-budget instruments are Austin, Danelectro, Encore, Jay Turser, Johnson, Lotus, and Rockwood. Their price lists typically start around two hundred dollars or even lower.

A bit higher

Others start a bit higher, and often include intermediate – and sometimes professional – instruments too. Examples are Aria, Aslin Dane, Brownsville, Cort, Dean, DeArmond, Fernandes, Framus, Hohner, LTD (related to ESP), Samick, and Tradition. Samick is one such manufacturer that builds instruments for various – Japanese, European, American – companies.

... and higher

Blade, Brawley, Burns, Carvin, Chandler, Godin, Maverick, and Schecter are a few examples of brands that you'll mainly find higher up in the budget range, throughout the intermediate price range; some are represented in the professional range as well.

Professional only

The number of guitar brands that specialize in the professional price range (list prices starting around fourteen or fifteen hundred dollars) is endless. A few of the better-known names include Alembic, Baker, Brian Moore, ESP, G&L, Modulus, Moonstone, Music Man, Parker, Paul Reed Smith, Rickenbacker, Sadowsky, Tom Anderson, Valley Arts, and Vigier. You could make a list of at least the same length mentioning names of hollow-body specialists, such as Benedetto, Höfner, Guild, Heritage, and Renaissance.

Basses only

Most specialized bass companies focus on the professional range. A few include instruments in the lower or intermediate price range too: Three examples are MTD, Spector, and Warwick.

Custom-made

There are many individual guitar or bass manufacturers whose names are not included in this chapter. To locate them, consult the magazines and other resources listed on pages 137–139. Note that some of the companies mentioned above offer custom-made instruments as well, allowing customers to choose from numerous types of woods, finishes, pickup configurations, necks, fingerboards…

Pickups and hardware

Many guitar makers, large and small, buy many of the components they use from other companies, rather than making them themselves. The same products are also often used to upgrade or revamp instruments. Some of the better-known pickup makers include **Joe Barden**, **Bartolini**, **EMG**, **Evans**, **DiMarzio**, **Lawrence**, **Lindy Fralin**, and **Seymour Duncan**. Major names in tuning machines and other hardware items include **Gotoh**, **Grover**, **Hipshot**, **Kluson**, **Schaller**, and **Sperzel**.

GLOSSARY AND INDEX

This glossary briefly explains all the jargon touched on so far. It also contains some words that haven't been mentioned yet, but which you may come across in other books, in magazines, or in catalogs. The numbers refer to the page(s) where the term is explained in this Tipbook.

Action *(107–109)* String height; the distance between the strings and the fingerboard.

Active EQ *(61–62)* Extended tone control, mostly used on bass guitars.

Active pickups *(62)* Active pickups produce a clean, noise-free signal. Can be used on basses and guitars.

Adjustment *(47–48, 107–113)* A well-adjusted guitar or bass sounds better and is easier to play.

Amplifiers *(12–14, 68, 69).*

Archtop *(10)* Instruments with an arched top; commonly used to indicate hollow-body instruments.

Binding *(7, 11)* A decorative and protective strip, running along the edge of the body or neck.

Bookmatched *(32, 124–125)* A bookmatched body or top is made from a single piece of wood which is split so that it can be folded open like a book.

Bout *(5, 7)* The shoulders and hips of the body are also known as the upper and lower bout.

Bridge *(5, 9, 10, 11, 39, 46–49)* The strings run from the tuning machines to the bridge which usually has individually adjustable bridge saddles to set string height and intonation.

Bridge pickup *(54)* The pickup closest to the bridge.

Bridge saddles See: *Saddles.*

Cables *(87–89)* Always have a spare one with you.

Coil *(54, 55)* Most pickups have one or two coils, *i.e.,* magnets with copper wire wound around them. See also: *Single-coil pickup* and *Humbucker.*

Coil-tap *(57)* A coil-tap alows you to make a hum-bucker act like a single-coil pickup.

Compound-wound strings *(75)* Strings with several windings.

Cutaway *(5, 6, 11)* Recessed part of the body; provides easier access to the higher frets.

Double-locking tremolo See: *Locking nut, lock-nut.*

D-tuner *(103)* Device which allows you to detune the low E-string to a D.

Dual-coil pickup See: *Humbucker.*

Effects *(14–15)* Most guitar players and many bassists use one or more effects to spice up their sound.

***f*-Hole guitar** Another name for arch-top guitar, which usually has two *f*-shaped sound holes.

Fingerboard *(5, 6, 11, 34–36, 39, 40, 65, 67)* When you play, you press the strings to the fingerboard. Also called *fretboard.*

Flat-wound *(75)* A string wound with a flat ribbon.

Floating *(10, 48)* Hollow-bodies often have a floating tailpiece, bridge, and pick-guard, and sometimes a floating pickup *(48–49)* too, which allows the guitar's top to resonate freely.

Four-conductor wiring Allows for alternative wiring combinations (*e.g.,* series, parallel, split-coil) of a humbucker.

Fretboard See: *Fingerboard.*

Fretless bass *(43)* A bass guitar without frets.

Frets *(5, 6, 11, 41–44)* The metal strips on the fingerboard or *fretboard.*

Hard-tail guitar See: *Tremolo.*

Hardware *(8–9)* The metal components of a guitar (bridge, tuning machines, etc.).

Hollowbody *(10–11, 32)* An electric guitar with a soundbox or resonance chamber. See also: *Solid-body* and *Archtop*.

Humbucker *(54–57, 60)* A dual-coil pickup, designed to 'buck the hum' often emitted by single-coil designs. Sounds thicker and warmer than a single-coil pickup.

Insurance *(114)* Smart.

Intonation *(109–112)* To be able to play in tune, the intonation of your instrument should be well-adjusted.

Locking nut, lock-nut *(50–51)* A clamp that fixes your strings at the nut; part of a *locking tremolo*. Also called top-lock. A *double-locking tremolo* also locks the strings at the bridge.

Locking tuning machines *(84)* Tuning machines which 'lock' the string in place.

Machine heads See: *Tuning machines.*

MIDI *(66)* Musical Instru-ment Digital Interface. Allows communication between electronic musical devices: You can use a MIDI-guitar to trigger a synthesizer, for example.

Neck *(5, 6, 33–34, 35, 38, 39)* Runs between the body and the head.

Neck pickup *(54)* The pickup closest to the neck.

Nut *(5, 9, 53, 102)* Small strip between the head and the fingerboard. Important for string spacing, action, tone, and tuning stability.

Open tuning *(104)* Another way of tuning your guitar.

Parallel *(60)* Pickups can be wired in parallel or *in series.*

Passive instruments Instruments without active electronics. See: *Active EQ* and *Active pickups.*

Phase *(60)* Humbuckers (or two single coils) can be wired in or out of phase.

Pickguard *(4, 5, 28)* Protects the body from being scratched by the pick or plectrum.

Pickup *(4, 5, 11, 53–57, 59–61, 62–67)* Picks up

the strings' vibrations and converts them into electrical signals.

Pickup selector *(5, 59–61)* Allows you to select the pickup(s) you want to use.

Piezo pickup *(62–63, 121)* Special type of pressure-sensitive pickup.

Plain strings *(7, 72)* The two or three unwound strings on a guitar. See also: *Wound strings.*

Position markers *(5, 6, 36)* Mark the 3rd, 5th, 7th, 9th, 12th (etc.) positions or frets on your instrument.

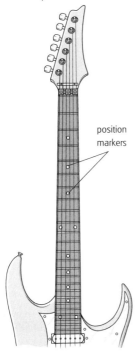

position markers

Pot, potentiometer *(59)* The electrical controls found under the volume and tone controls. A *trim pot* is a small pot that is normally mounted inside the instrument's control cavity.

Radius *(34–35)* Indicates the exact curvature of the fingerboard.

Reverse headstock*(38)* A reverse headstock makes the treble strings shorter, and the bass strings longer, affecting both sound and playability.

Round-wound *(75)* String wound with a thin, rounded wire. See also: *Flat-wound.*

Saddles *(5, 9, 47–48, 108)* Most bridges have individually adjustable saddles to set intonation, action, and (sometimes) string spacing.

Scale *(40–41)* Double the distance from the nut to the 12th fret. Important for the sound and the playability of the instrument.

Semi-hollow, semi-solid *(10, 31, 122)* Confusing terms, used to refer to a variety of guitars that have one or more pickups, a large or a shallow soundbox, or one or two small resonance chambers.

Series See: *Parallel.*

Single-coil pickup *(55–57, 60)* Produces a brighter, cleaner, tighter sound than a dual-coil pickup or humbucker. See also: *Humbucker.*

Soundbox *(10, 116, 122)* The hollow 'box' or chamber that acoustically amplifies the sound of an acoustic instrument.

Staggered pickups *(64, 65)* Pickups with pole pieces at varying heights.

Staggered tuning machines *(46)* Tuning machines with posts of varying lengths.

Stop tailpiece, stopbar tailpiece *(9, 47)* A separate tailpiece, mounted on the instrument's top.

String height See: *Action.*

String pull *(64, 112–113)* Effect caused by too strong pickup magnets or badly adjusted pickups, disturbing the strings' vibrations.

String tree *(5, 38–39, 46, 50)* Holds down the thinner strings so they don't buzz at, or pop out of the nut.

String winder *(82)* Speeds up (un)winding strings.

Strings *(5, 7–8, 72–78, 79–86).*

Tailpiece *(5, 9, 10, 11, 47, 48, 50)* On some instruments, the strings are attached to a *tailpiece*, instead of to the bridge.

Thinline *(10)* Hollowbody with a shallow soundbox. Also called *slimline*.

Through-neck *(37, 125)* A full-length neck that extends down the body to the tail.

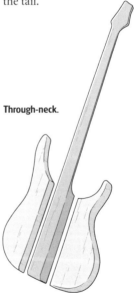

Through-neck.

Tilted headstock *(38–39)* A (backward) tilted headstock eliminates the need for string trees.

Toggle switch *(59)* Usually a three-way pickup selector (1. neck pickup; 2. both pickups; 3. bridge pickup). Also known as *leaf switch*.

Tremolo system *(9, 49–53, 71, 109, 110)* A bridge or tailpiece with an arm (the *tremolo bar*) that allows you to alter the tension of your strings by bending the pitch up or down. Also called *vibrato* (which is one of the effects you actually produce with a 'tremolo'), or *whammy*. A *tremolo guitar* is a guitar with a trem; a hard-tail guitar is one without.

Trim pot See: *Pot, potentiometer.*

Truss rod *(6, 37)* Adjustable rod(s) in the neck. The truss rod counteracts the strings' tension.

Tuner *(94–98)* 1. Electronic device that helps you tune. 2. See: *Tuning machine.*

Tuning machines *(5, 8, 11, 44–46)* Open, closed, or sealed machines to tune your strings with. Also called *tuners*, (*tuning*) *gears*, (*tuning*) *pegs*, or *machine heads*.

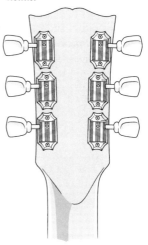

Tuning machines.

Vibrato, vibrato unit See: *Tremolo.*

Waist See: *Bout.*

Whammy See: *Tremolo.*

Wound strings *(7, 8, 72, 74, 75)* The thickest three or four guitar strings and all bass strings are wound with metal wire or ribbon, allowing them to sound their proper pitches.

Zero fret *(42)* Extra fret, close to the nut.

TIPCODE LIST

The Tipcodes in this book offer easy access to short movies, photo series, soundtracks, and other additional information at www.tipbook.com. For your convenience, the Tipcodes in this Tipbook have been listed below.

Tipcode	Topic	Page	Chapter
EGTR-001	String pitches guitar: E, A, D, G, B, E	**7**	2
EGTR-002	String pitches bass: E, A, D, G	**7**	2
EGTR-003	Tremolo: vibrato and pitch bend	**9, 49**	2, 5
EGTR-004	Clean and distorted	**13**	2
EGTR-005	Effects	**15**	2
EGTR-006	Fretted & fretless bass guitar	**43**	5
EGTR-007	Bridge and neck pickups	**54**	5
EGTR-008	Humbucker and single-coil pickup	**55**	5
EGTR-009	Fitting new strings at the tuning machines	**82**	7
EGTR-010	Stabilizing strings	**85**	7
EGTR-011	String pitches guitar (reference pitches)	**94**	9
EGTR-012	String pitches bass (reference pitches)	**94**	9
EGTR-013	A=440	**97**	9
EGTR-014	Tuning: string to string	**98**	9
EGTR-015	Tuning fork	**99**	9
EGTR-016	Tuning with harmonics	**100**	9
EGTR-017	Beats	**100**	9
EGTR-018	Adjusting intonation	**110**	10
EGTR-019	Moving saddle; pitch changes	**110**	10
EGTR-020	Double bass	**120**	12
EGTR-021	Classical and steel-string guitars	**120**	12
EGTR-022	Making an electric guitar	**124**	13

WANT TO KNOW MORE?

Tipbooks supply you with basic information on the instrument of your choice and everything that comes with it. Of course, there's a lot more to be found on all subjects you came across on these pages. A selection of magazines, books, websites, and newsgroups.

MAGAZINES

The magazines listed below concentrate on electric guitars, basses, or both; some include acoustic models as well. Please note that this list is not intended to be complete.

- *Bass Player*, USA, phone (800) 234-1831 or (650) 513-4300, www.bassplayer.com, bassplayer@neodata.com.
- *Bassics*, USA, phone (310) 370-1695, www.bassics.com.
- *Guitar Digest*, USA, phone (740) 797 3351, www.guitardigest.com.
- *Guitar One*, USA, phone (212) 561-3000, www.guitaronemag.com.
- *Guitar Player*, USA, (800) 289-9839 or (650) 513-4300, www.guitarplayer.com, guitarplayer@neodata.com.
- *Guitar World*, USA, phone (800) 866-2886 or (850) 682-7644, www.guitarworld.com.
- *Women Who Rock*, phone (212) 561-3000, www.womenwhorockmag.com.

International magazines

- *Australian Guitar Magazine*, phone +61 (0)2 9699-0333, ausguitar@next.com.au.
- *Guitarist*, UK, phone +44 1225 442244, www.guitarist.co.uk

All data in this section are subject to change.

- *Total Guitar*, UK, phone +44 1225 442244, www.totalguitar.co.uk
- *Guitar Techniques*, phone +44 1225 442244, www.futurenet.co.uk
- *What Guitar?*, phone +44 1225 442244, www.futurenet.co.uk
- *Guitar*, phone +44 (0)20 8744 0600, guitar@ipcmedia.com
- *Guitar Buyer*, phone +44 (0) 1954 252 983, mb.media@btopenworld.com

BOOKS

There are dozens of books on guitars and basses, including publications that focus on a specific brand, a specific era, or any other subject. The following is a very limited selection.

- *The Complete Guitarist*, Richard Chapman (Dorling Kindersley, 1994; 191 pages; ISBN 1 564 58711 8).
- *The Guitar Handbook*, Ralph Denyer (Knopf, 1992; 256 pages; ISBN 0 679 74275 1).
- *The Ultimate Guitar Book*, Tony Bacon (Knopf, 1997; 192 pages; ISBN 0 375 70090 0).
- *Picks! – The Colorful Saga of Vintage Celluloid Guitar Plectrums*, by Will Hoover (Backbeat Books, 1995; 107 pages; ISBN 0 879 30377 8).
- *Complete Guide to Guitar and Amp Maintenance – A Practical Manual for Every Guitar Player*, Ritchie Flieger (Hal Leonard, 1995; 80 pages; ISBN 0 793 53490 9).
- *Gruhn's Guide to Vintage Guitars – An Identification Guide for American Fretted Instruments*, George Gruhn, Walter Carter (Backbeat Books, 1999; 581 pages; ISBN 0 879 30422 7).
- *American Guitars – An Illustrated History*, Tom Wheeler (Harper Collins, 1992; 384 pages; ISBN 0 062 73154 8).
- *The Bonehead's Guide to Guitars*, Dominic Hilton (Hal Leonard, 2000; 80 pages; ISBN 0 7935 9799 4).
- *How To Make Your Electric Guitar Play Great!*, Dan Erlewine (Backbeat Books, 2001; 133 pages; ISBN 0 87930 601 7).
- *The Bass Book – A Complete Illustrated History of Bass Guitars*, Barry Moorhouse and Tony Bacon (Backbeat Books; 1995; ISBN 0 87930 368 9).

- *Electric Guitars – The Illustrated History*, Tony Bacon (Thunder Bay Press, 2000; 320 pages; ISBN 1 57145 281 8).
- *Blue Book of Electric Guitars*, S. P. Fjestad (Blue Book Publications, 2001, seventh edition; 928 pages; ISBN 1 88676 826 9).

INTERNET

The Internet offers lots information about guitars and basses. The following sites are good starting points, offering both information and links to other sites:

- activebass.com
- basslinks.com
- electric-guitars.net
- electricbass.com
- guitar.about.com
- guitar.about.com/cs/bass
- guitar.com
- guitarlinks.com
- guitarnotes.com
- guitarnuts.com
- guitarsite.com
- magpie.com/tbl
- talkbass.com
- wholenote.com

OTHER TIPBOOKS

Among the other Tipbooks that you may find of interest is *Tipbook Music on Paper*, which tells you basically everything you need to know about sheet music and music theory: reading notes, dynamic markings, articulation signs, and so on. This book, illustrated with numerous easily playable examples, teaches you to read music in a couple of chapters. It's also a highly accessible reference book, should you need to brush up on transposing, the circle of fifths, scales, and much more. Two more Tipbooks that may be of interest are *Tipbook Acoustic Guitar* and – in the future – *Tipbook Amplifiers & Effects*.

ESSENTIAL DATA

In the event of your equipment being stolen or lost, or if you decide to sell it, it's useful to have all the relevant data at hand. Here are two pages to list everything you need – for the insurance, for the police, for a prospective buyer, or just for yourself.

INSURANCE

Insurance company:

Phone: Fax:

E-mail:

Contact person:

Phone: Fax:

E-mail:

Policy number: Cost:

INSTRUMENTS, AMPS, EFFECTS

Make and model:

Serial number:

Color: Price:

Purchase date:

Place of purchase:

Phone: Fax:

Website: E-mail:

Make and model:

Serial number:

Color: Price:

Purchase date:

Place of purchase:

Phone: Fax:

Website:

Make and model:

Serial number:

Color: Price:

Purchase date:

Place of purchase:

Phone: Fax:

Website:

STRINGS

If you list the stings you're currently using, you'll later be able to buy the same ones if you like them, or different ones if you don't. Making a note of when you put them on helps you remember how long they last.

Make: Type:

Gauge/Tension: Date:

Comments:

Make: Type:

Gauge/Tension: Date:

Comments:

Make: Type:

Gauge/Tension: Date:

Comments:

Make: Type:

Gauge/Tension: Date:

Comments:

Make: Type:

Gauge/Tension: Date:

Comments: